Terrific Tips

FOR PRESCHOOL TEACHERS

By Barbara F. Backer
Illustrated by Priscilla Burris

 Totline® Publications
A Division of Frank Schaffer Publications, Inc.
Torrance, California

To teachers everywhere. May these tips help you enrich children's lives.

—B.F.B.

Managing Editor: Kathleen Cubley

Editor: Susan Hodges

Contributing Editors: Gayle Bittinger, Elizabeth McKinnon, Susan Sexton, Jean Warren

Copyeditor: Kris Fulsaas

Proofreader: Miriam Bulmer

Graphic Designer (Interior): Sarah Ness

Layout Artist: Gordon Frazier

Graphic Designer (Cover): Brenda Mann Harrison

Production Managers: Jo Anna Haffner, Melody Olney

Terrific Tips for Preschool Teachers is a compilation and revision of these Totline Publications materials: WPH 4007 *Creating Theme Environments*; WPH 4008 *Encouraging Creativity*; WPH 4009 *Developing Motor Skills*; WPH 4010 *Developing Language Skills*; WPH 4011 *Teaching Basic Concepts*; and WPH 4012 *Spicing Up Learning Centers*.

ISBN: 1-57029-236-1

Library of Congress Catalog Card Number 98-60800

Printed in the United States of America

Published by Totline Publications

Business Office: 23740 Hawthorne Blvd.
Torrance, CA 90505

Contents

Encouraging Creativity

Art

Young children enjoy the process of creating with art materials, but they have little interest in the finished product. They appreciate opportunities to explore art materials in their own ways. Encourage all attempts at manipulating materials, and avoid art experiences that have a heavy emphasis on a final product.

1 The world around us comes in all colors, shapes, and sizes. Always provide your children with a variety of materials so their artwork can be as unique as their world. Include an assortment of papers, paints, and writing materials. Remember to include flesh-toned colors that represent all of the children in your care. Accept all artistic efforts and let the children know there are many ways to create beauty.

2 Challenge creative thinking. Ask your children how many ways they can put paint on paper. Exchange paintbrushes for twigs, pipe cleaners, pine cones, feather dusters, crumpled paper, scrunched-up fabric, sponges, or spray bottles. Encourage all efforts.

3 When a child says, "I can't draw," show him or her pictures of modern art. You'll find these in books at the library. In Piet Mondrian's blocks of color and Jackson Pollock's splashing and dribbling techniques, your children will see artwork with the freshness of their own. Discuss the works with them. Ask, "How could you make something like that?" Display the books in the art center, and provide materials for the children who are inspired by these modern art techniques.

4 Have your children make a ceiling mural on butcher paper to look at during rest time. Let them brainstorm ideas of restful colors and designs. Perhaps they'll sponge-paint white clouds on sky blue paper, or "grow" a field of spattered wildflower shapes. For a night sky, they might spatter white and gold paint across a dark background.

5 Clay is a medium that changes shape and form easily. These changes challenge a child's creative thinking as each change suggests a new idea. Provide a variety of clays at different times throughout the year. Modeling dough, potter's clay, and cornstarch dough each offer a different tactile experience.

8 To add variety and interest to fingerpainting, provide gadgets for your children to press into or drag through the paint. You may wish to try cookie cutters, combs, cardboard tubes, straws, a feather duster, interlocking plastic blocks, or other small, washable toys.

9 When weather allows, paint outside. Show your children how to drip and splash paint onto paper. To drip paint, let paint drizzle off the bristles onto the paper. To splash paint, dip a brush in paint, hold it with the bristles up, then snap the wrist to make your paint spatter on the paper. Children love this technique, which adds stars to the sky or sunlight sparkles to ocean water.

6 Children love to make their own modeling dough. Provide measuring cups, separate bowls of flour and salt, a small pitcher of water, and a medicine dropper in a bowl of cooking oil. Help your children measure and combine three parts flour, one part salt, one part water, and a few drops of oil.

7 Demonstrate and practice clay-handling techniques with the following song.

Sung to: "The Wheels on the Bus"

I use my hands to roll the clay,
Roll the clay, roll the clay.
I use my hands to roll the clay,
Roll, roll, roll the clay.

Additional verses: I use my hands to pound the clay; squeeze the clay; mash the clay. Ask your children to make up their own verses.

Barbara Backer

10 Children take more creative risks when they know the results aren't permanent. They love to draw on chalkboards and use erasers. Part of the fun of drawing with chalk on sidewalks is watching the creations fade away. Or hang up a clear shower curtain and offer your children washable markers to draw on it with. They can erase their work with a damp rag.

Language

Children are naturally creative thinkers. But too often that creativity is dampened when young ones give voice to their ideas, and adults dismiss those thoughts as silly or "wrong." Such children begin to doubt their original ideas and may stop contributing. Let your children know that all ideas are respected in your room. Provide them with these and other opportunities to explore language.

1 Change the words to familiar rhymes and songs. Substitute your children's names for those of nursery rhyme characters, and encourage the children to think of their own variations, as in the following example.

Linus be nimble,
Linus be quick.
Linus jump over
The dinosaur puppet.

Barbara Backer

2 To encourage creative language, read, then discuss, the story of Cinderella, who rode in a coach made from a pumpkin. Children enjoy imagining how other characters might travel. What would Mary's lamb ride in? Where would she go? What about Goldilocks?

3 Show your children a doll and a small suitcase. Say, "This doll has packed her suitcase. Where do you think she is going?" Ask the children why the doll is going there and what she will do when she gets to her destination. Who will travel with her? What did she pack in the suitcase?

4 Preschoolers often create rhymes and stories while playing. Jot down or tape record these rhymes and read them back during group time.

5 Sometimes communication is nonverbal. Children already recognize many hand signals, including "Come here," "Wait a minute," and "Shhh." What signs can your children create for their group's communication needs? Can they think of signals for "It's time to go outside," "Let's clean up," or "Please sit down"? Later, explain that people who cannot hear communicate through sign language. Borrow a book of American Sign Language from the library and teach the children a few simple signs.

6 Children use new vocabulary as they act out other roles. To stimulate language development, make a microphone by covering a toilet tissue tube with aluminum foil. Tape a crumpled foil ball to the top. Use the microphone for news show interviews. Model for your children how they can pretend to be someone else. "Today we have as our guest Baby Bear. He and his family had an unusual surprise today when they returned from their walk in the woods. Can you tell us what happened, Baby Bear?" Capture these interviews on tape so the children can enjoy them again and again.

7 Children who love fairy tales enjoy making up stories of their own. After reading a familiar tale, such as "Goldilocks and the Three Bears," encourage your children to develop their own version. Ask questions to spark their imagination: "What would happen if Goldilocks were a boy? If the three bears were gerbils?" Write down the children's ideas as they say them, and read the new version of the story to them.

8 Nonsense rhymes celebrate the joy of language. Substitute nonsense words for other words in favorite nursery rhymes. Introduce this nonsense variation of "Hickory, Dickory, Dock."

Fliberty, liberty block.
The flub ran up the rock.
The rock flim-flammed.
The flub blim-blammed.
Fliberty, liberty block.

Barbara Backer

9 Collect postcards with interesting pictures, and keep them on hand for impromptu language fun. Let each of your children choose a card and tell a story about the picture.

10 Fantasy games stretch children's imaginations and develop problem-solving skills. The "What If?" game is a great one. Ask your children what they would do if they could fly, if their house were made of cheese, if they had a dog who disliked baths, or if they were a parent whose child didn't want to go to bed. Think of a new question each day.

Dramatics

Before the age of 1, children begin creative dramatic play when they hand you a toy cup and wait for you to pretend to drink. Dramatic play is natural for them. Take advantage of every opportunity to include creative dramatics in your room.

3 Practice moving like characters in a story. How did the three bears move through their house after their walk in the woods? How did the billy goats move across the bridge? Did the biggest goat move differently from the smallest? How did Jack move when he climbed up the beanstalk? When he ran down with the giant following him?

4 Challenge your children to dramatize inanimate objects. Be a telephone. What happens if no one is there to answer you? Find a partner to be your answering machine. You are bread and someone has just put you in a toaster. You are an iron. How do you move? What happens if someone pulls your plug?

5 Our movements often reveal our emotions. Help your children think about how they move when they are excited, happy, angry, or sad. Encourage them to use their whole bodies. Have volunteers show an emotion through movement (give suggestions as necessary) and let others in the group guess the emotion.

1 When you act out familiar stories, remember that more than one child can act out each role, all at the same time. Why can't we have three trolls, six big goats, two middle-size goats, and four little goats?

2 Dramatize nursery rhymes, chants, and the lyrics of songs you've learned at music time. Add simple props and act out songs while you sing them.

6 Most children believe in magic. Make a magic wand for creative activities by rolling a chopstick in glue and dipping it in glitter. Wave the wand over your children to "turn them into" goopy gelatin, buzzing bees, lazy elephants, or other imaginary creatures. Give each child a chance to use the wand.

7 Props add another dimension to dramatic play. Collect props related to a theme and store them in prop boxes. Label these with pictures and put them within easy reach of your children. For a picnic box, you might include a tablecloth, plastic plates and utensils, a picnic basket, and an empty spray bottle labeled: Bug Spray. A chef's box might include a rolling pin, an apron, pans, bowls, and wooden spoons.

8 Children enjoy creating their own plays. Older children can dictate simple dialogue to be written on chart paper. Encourage your children to make costumes from items in the housekeeping center or from lengths of fabric held in place with clothespins.

9 Your children can build a simple stage from large hollow blocks, set up chairs theater-style, make tickets and advertising posters, and "write" invitations to other groups to see their performance. Remember, this is their production, and spontaneity is important.

10 For a relaxing end to dramatic play, have your children imagine they are syrup in a bottle. Someone picks up the bottle and slowly they are poured onto a stack of warm pancakes. They spread across, then they slowly sink into the first pancake, then the next, and the next. They slowly sink deeper and deeper until they are little puddles on the plate.

Construction

Construction differs from drawing and other creative activities because from the beginning, a child's creations are usually representational. Children build with a product in mind. To foster creative construction, give your children plenty of time to experiment with different materials and structures. Whenever possible, allow the children to work on a project until they finish it.

1 Use baskets to distribute construction materials to a small group of children. Put a few plastic animals, cardboard tubes, and interlocking blocks in each basket. Challenge your children to build something the animals can use.

2 Read a favorite story, then ask your children to build something they saw in the book. For instance, for "The Three Billy Goats Gruff," they can build a bridge. Use teddy bear counters or other plastic figures to act out stories in these new environments.

3 Hang pictures in your block center to stimulate creative thinking and building. Look for pictures of unusual people, places, and things to spark your children's imaginations. Change pictures often and file in a box the ones that aren't on display, so the children can use them freely.

4 Collect small props related to various themes, and store each set in a separate basket. Keep these in your block center, and change baskets often to promote variety in your children's play. For instance, you might assemble an airport basket containing plastic airplanes, airport signs, and suitcases made of match boxes, or a circus basket containing clown counters, small plastic animals, circus pictures, and plastic bracelets to use as circus rings.

5 Children respond creatively when offered unusual materials. Ask parents to help you collect small, empty cardboard boxes. Have each of your children select about six boxes to glue together to make a construction. Cover the work area completely with newspaper or a drop cloth, and be prepared for lots of dripping glue as the children try many possibilities. Allow several days for these creations to dry.

8 Add a basket of empty plastic soda bottles, bottle tops, and jar lids to the block or carpentry centers. Provide fabric strips and large flat pieces of cardboard or wood for your children to incorporate into their creations.

9 Providing a variety of block sizes and types stimulates creative construction. Make lightweight, sturdy blocks by stuffing empty laundry detergent boxes and oatmeal boxes with crumpled newspaper. Glue shut. Cover with self-stick paper, if desired.

10 Give each of your children a variety of unit blocks. Empty the block shelves so each child will have plenty of blocks. Have the children lay three of their blocks on the floor. Now, challenge them to build upward from there. Only those three blocks should touch the floor. Demonstrate this several times and be aware that some children won't understand the concept. Take pictures of the creations. Repeat the activity several times during the year and take photographs to record the children's progress.

6 Help your children connect their creative constructions with real experiences. Display souvenir items from field trips—brochures, photos, postcards, paper hats, tongue depressors—in the block area to spark ideas. Add props to stimulate creativity: a short length of garden hose after a trip to the fire station; grocery bags after a trip to the supermarket; toy animals after a farm visit.

7 Remove all curved blocks from the Block Center, and challenge your children to build with only straight-edge blocks. On another day, offer only curved blocks. How are constructions different on these days? Take snapshots of each day's constructions and discuss them.

Inventions

1 Encourage your children to invent a toy for the room. Can they invent something for the sand table? For the water table? For the block center? Can they create a doll to play with and clothes for it to wear?

2 Give your children cardboard tubes of various lengths and strips of masking tape, and then challenge them to make shapes. Some will make standard shapes; others will invent new shapes. Can they create names for these shapes? Take snapshots of the shapes and put the photos into a photo album or on a bulletin board. Label each shape and name its creator.

3 Set out pictures of cars, minivans, trucks, and buses. Discuss their differences and similarities. Challenge your children to make vehicles for the block center, using egg cartons that have been precut crosswise into two-seaters, four-seaters, and eight-seaters. Provide markers, twist ties, and other items for the children to use in their creations.

4 Challenge your children to invent a musical instrument from a variety of materials, including plastic bottles, yogurt containers, boxes, buttons, rubber bands, and yarn. Make fancy headbands and have a parade!

5 Offer your children a large selection of throwaways and craft items. What can they make with just three of these items? With five? With six?

6 Include paper clips, brass paper fasteners, rubber bands, paper punches, small wooden wheels, and spools in your selection of craft items and throwaways. Challenge your children to invent something with moving parts.

7 Discuss jobs that have to be done regularly: taking out trash, washing dishes, making beds, feeding pets. Have your children draw pictures of inventions that might do these jobs.

8 Provide brass paper fasteners, glue, and many construction paper shapes, including long strips. Let your children use the materials to make a machine. Have them name the machine and tell what it can do.

9 Challenge older children to invent machines (by drawing or building) that could solve problems from storybooks. For instance, you might ask them to make a machine that could get the Three Billy Goats Gruff across the river without using the bridge.

10 Give your children only a few items, such as cardboard tubes, yarn, and tape, and see what they devise. Sometimes a limited supply of materials promotes imagination.

Problem Solving with Manipulatives

Children develop abstract thinking skills when they use tools to help solve problems. Anything can serve as a tool. Use your own creativity to add to this list of ways for using manipulatives to solve problems.

1 Children like to build ramps from blocks and roll trucks down them. Use this interest to stimulate problem solving. With tape, mark on the floor the distance the trucks have traveled, then challenge your children to make ramps that make the trucks go farther. What do they conclude?

2 Tubes are great problem-solving tools. Give your children cardboard tubes or sections of PVC pipe. Add small balls and marbles, and watch as the children begin rolling them through the tubes. Ask the children how they could make the marbles roll through faster or slower. What might make them roll farther when they exit the tube? Does it matter whether the tube is long or short? Thick or thin?

3 Help your children discover why some of their block structures fall down. Have them build two block structures—one with a broad base, and one with a narrow base. Which is sturdier? Which is easier to knock down?

4 Take advantage of opportunities to show your children how manipulatives can become tools to help us simplify our work. Spill a large container of paper clips over a wide area. Demonstrate how to use a magnet to pick up the clips. Whenever you spill nails, paper clips, or other magnetic items, let the children use magnets to clean up the spill.

5 Introduce your children to the concept of graphing through the following activity. Survey the children to find out how many have a pet and how many do not. Instead of counting the children, have each take a counting cube. Ask children with pets to take a red cube, and those without pets to take a blue one. Gather and stack the cubes by color. Which stack is higher? How many children have pets? How did the cubes help you?

6 Help your children use egg timers to solve conflicts over how long a child may take a turn with a popular toy.

7 Challenge your children's thinking skills with a memory game. Have a child sit with a partner as you place three bottle caps on the rug. Ask the first child to hide his or her eyes while the other child puts none, one, two, or all three caps under an overturned margarine tub. The first child looks at the remaining caps and must guess how many caps are under the tub. Have the children take turns hiding and guessing.

8 Show your children how wheels help us move heavy things. Fill a box with books and let the children attempt to move it across the room. They may discover that sliding the box is easier than carrying it. Now put a number of dowels under the box. Have the children slowly roll the box across the dowels, moving the dowels from the back to the front as the box moves off them. Discuss what happened. Think about how a wagon or a car could move if it had no wheels.

9 Have your children use manipulatives to measure distance. Place two items on the floor. Show your children how to lay a line of craft sticks between the items and count the sticks to discover the distance. Let them compare this distance to other distances in the room. Challenge your children to find other standard-size items with which to measure. Felt tip markers, unit blocks, and straws are just a few of the possibilities.

10 Plastic figures, counting cubes, and other manipulatives are perfect for estimation activities. Float a plastic food tray in the water table. Ask your children to predict how many plastic figures the tray will hold before it sinks. Let them test their predictions. Then have the children repeat the activity with a different item.

Cooking

All recipes are the creative results of an inventive cook using ingredients in a new way. Stimulate children's creativity in the kitchen by providing many healthy ingredients and allowing children to use them in their own way. There's more than one right way to make a pizza, a sandwich, and most everything else.

1 Children enjoy making their own individual pizzas. Let your children spread spaghetti sauce on an English muffin and choose from an assortment of toppings, such as sliced mushrooms, sliced cherry tomatoes, chopped green pepper, and sliced olives. Sprinkle grated mozzarella or cheddar cheese on top and brown in a toaster oven.

2 Create a snack to complement your study of things that sink and things that float. For each child, pour $\frac{1}{4}$ to $\frac{1}{2}$ cup liquid gelatin into a clear-plastic cup. Let your children choose ingredients to add to their gelatin. Offer a selection of small chunks of fruit, pretzel pieces, and marshmallows. Have each child add his or her choices, then place the cups in the refrigerator to chill. Have the children compare finished creations. What sank to the bottom of the gelatin? What floated on top? What is "swimming" in between?

3 Encourage your children to think of creative names for the foods they eat. With a bit of imagination, macaroni and cheese might become "golden straws" and egg salad "dinosaur egg salad."

4 Children enjoy creating food sculptures using peanut butter as glue. Using a cracker as a base, have your children spread on peanut butter, then add other items to build an edible creation. Try round and square cereal pieces, raisins, seeds, and shredded carrot. What other original ideas do the children have?

5 Tint cream cheese with a few drops of food coloring—orange at Halloween, green at Christmas, red or pink for Valentine's Day, pastel colors in spring. Have your children use cookie cutters to cut shapes from toasted bread. Let them spread on the cream cheese with butter knives, then add raisins or sunflower seeds for decorations. Use shredded carrots and alfalfa sprouts as hair or fur for funny face and monster creations.

8 Offer a selection of healthy foods that can be eaten with hands: bologna cut in quarters, cheese cut in quarters, sliced pickles, sliced cucumber, sliced carrot, bread, crackers, etc. Let each of your children choose three items and invent a snack that has a top, a middle, and a bottom.

9 Give your children the opportunity to create menus and prepare foods for each other. Once a week select a small committee of three or four children to plan the next day's snack. On the next day let them fix and serve the snack (with your help and supervision).

10 Children feel proud and important when they can prepare healthy snacks for their families. Help them learn to fix snacks the whole family can enjoy. Send home a note and a list of ingredients asking parents to let the children create family snacks.

6 Children develop autonomy when they are offered choices. Let your children create their own snacks. Offer choices of healthy raw vegetables for making small salads, cereals and dried fruits for creating snack mixes, and crackers and spreads for an appetizer. Offer only two or three choices early in the year (carrot sticks and a choice of two dips; round or square cereal pieces and raisins). Add more choices as the year progresses.

7 Have your children create fruit kabobs. Provide bamboo skewers, sliced bananas, seedless grapes, and cubed fruit. Have the children thread the fruit onto the skewers in any combination they desire.

Making Up Games

Children learn a lot from playing games—counting, adding, subtracting, matching, paying attention, cooperating, taking turns, waiting a turn. They especially enjoy inventing their own games. Support your children's efforts by providing an assortment of materials for game making.

1 You can stimulate your children's creative thinking by challenging them to make up a racing game. Ask how they will make the track. What will race around the track? Where will the start be? The finish?

2 Children can work on skills like color matching and counting while they invent games. Have your children bring favorite classroom items to small group meetings. Can they make up a color matching game using these items? How many items will they try to match by color? How many matching colors do they have?

3 Have your children help you make up games about finding things that are the same in one way, but not all ways. For example, find things that are the same shape, but not the same size: teacher's hand and child's hand, a marble and a beach ball, a crayon box and a table top. Find things that are the same thing, but not the same color: two crayons, two markers, two coats. Find things that are the same color, but not the same thing: yellow towel and yellow truck; red ball and red crayon. What other variations can the children discover?

4 Buy old gameboards and pieces at garage sales. They don't need to be complete. Let your children combine the boards and pieces to invent new games.

5 Pair your children. Give each child a toy car, and give each pair some unit blocks and dice. Can the pair use the blocks to make a pathway on the floor like a board game? Have them designate the start and finish and decide which direction to move.

9 Preschoolers do best with games that have few rules and no losers. Prevent conflict by promoting games where everyone wins.

10 The most enjoyable games are spontaneous ones. Be alert for opportunities to make up new games and adapt old favorites. By being flexible, you create an atmosphere in which creativity flourishes. But games are fun only when your children want to play them. Look for signs that a child is tired of a game, and be ready with a different activity.

6 A deck of playing cards can provide hours of creative fun. When purchasing cards, make sure each deck has a different picture on the back. This makes it easier to sort the cards and to put them away. The backs of the cards can be used for sorting and matching games as well.

7 Movement games are the perfect way to release pent-up energy on a rainy day. When your children are stuck indoors, set out some supplies and challenge them to make up a game that has movement, but not too much noise.

8 Games can be played anywhere—even in the sand area. Provide children with cans or small buckets to mold sand. Add a ball and encourage them to make up a game. Children who have been to the bowling alley will have immediate ideas about knocking down the cans and towers with the ball.

Outdoor Play

Take advantage of every opportunity to play outside. Children need vigorous activities to build their muscles and coordination, and to reduce stress.

3 Cardboard cartons are inexpensive (and often free) props for creative play. Cut a doorway into a large appliance box, and put the box on the playground. Your children might use it as a hideaway, a cave, a ship, an automobile, or anything else they imagine. Offer felt tip pens so they can label and decorate their special place.

4 Just a word or two from you can spark your children's outdoor creativity. Before going outside, announce: "Today when we go through this door, we will all be under water." The children may become sea horses, octopuses, and fish of all sorts and sizes. On other days, ask the children, "Where will we be when we go through this door?" You may find yourself in space, in dinosaur times, at the circus, or as part of an ice-skating show!

1 The outdoors offers many sounds that promote creativity. Sit outside with eyes closed. What do your children hear? Make a list, then let the children pick a sound and act out its source.

2 Support literacy and creative outdoor play by bringing markers and large scraps of paper and cardboard outside. Your children can make signs (with your help, if necessary), label areas (Monster's Cave, Toll Booth, Pirate Ship), or draw treasure maps. What else can they think of?

8 Chasing games are popular with young children, but most children can't tolerate being "out" for very long. Adapt these games so that waiting is kept to a minimum. Establish "free zones" where your children can observe without being chased.

9 In warm weather, water play goes outside, eliminating worries about spills or splashes. To make an instant water station, turn milk crates upside down and place plastic dishpans on them. Add soapy water and plain water to the dishpans, and put sponges and scrub brushes in each. Your children will find all sorts of things to wash, leaving your building, walkways, fence, tree trunks, and the whole outdoors cleaner than ever.

5 Your children can develop hand-eye coordination and large and small muscles by using large pieces of fabric and spring-type clothespins you provide. The children will think of many ways to use these. They may use the fabric to simulate a river, a lake, or a waterfall on the lawn, or to partition the jungle gym into rooms.

6 Collect a variety of outdoor play equipment, but don't use everything all at once. Change equipment often to keep your children's play fresh.

7 Children love to imitate animals. Help your children to make up outdoor games that include animal movements and sounds. One day they might decide to be farm animals, the next, creatures of the jungle.

10 Old tires are wonderful props for creative play. Children pretend they are prehistoric people as they roll tires from place to place. They work together stacking tires to create castle towers or a hideout. Obtain used tires from any shop that sells new ones or retreads. (Avoid steel belted tires; they contain pieces of metal.) If you drill holes in the tires, they won't collect rain water. Often a parent will help you find tires or drill the holes.

Teaching Basic Concepts

Numbers

1 Numbers are everywhere, and opportunities for learning math concepts surround us. Make counting a part of every day. Count the steps as you go up and down, the doors you pass through, the number of stirs or shakes in cooking, and the number of berries you put in the pancakes. How many crayons will you use? Watch as your children's interest in numbers grows.

2 Fill your classroom with materials that support mathematical learning. In addition to commercial manipulatives and number lines, include measuring cups, clocks, thermometers, and rulers for measuring; and buttons, bolts, dried beans, and egg cartons for counting and sorting.

3 Use mathematical terms in your conversations with your children. "You have the square block and Jasmine has the rectangle. The red crayon is longer than the blue. Sydney is first in line. Eric is second. Patrick is last."

4 Invite your children to make a cooperative number book for each number you study. Each child contributes a page to the book. He or she decides which picture to make. For a *Three* book, a child might draw (or paste on) three rainbows, three dinosaurs, or three swings. Compile the drawings and add a construction paper cover. Place the *Three* book in your group's reading area.

5 Combine counting and singing in the following game. Put a long piece of tape on the floor to make a line. Choose one of your children to stand on the line, and sing the following song as a group. At the end of each verse, let the last child choose another child to join him or her on the line. Continue adding children, then count backward as one child at a time leaves the line.

Sung to: "The Farmer in the Dell"

One child on the line.
One child on the line.
Heigh ho, the derry-oh,
One child on the line.

Additional verses: Two children on the line; three children; etc.

Barbara Backer

6 Make simple number games from die-cut paper shapes (available at parent-teacher stores). Write a different numeral on each of eight shapes. Have your children place the corresponding number of objects on each shape. Try using shapes that relate to your learning themes. For instance, the children might put plastic-foam "peanuts" on elephant shapes or feathers on bird shapes.

7 Books about mathematical concepts show children that numbers are a part of everyday life. Include counting books, simple cookbooks, advertising circulars, and other number books in your language center.

8 To help your children practice counting, make a gameboard by laying out a pathway of stickers on a 12-by-18-inch piece of posterboard. Mark the starting place and the finish. For older children, include one or two "shortcuts" along the way, as shown in the illustration. The children roll a die and move colored bottle caps the number of spaces indicated.

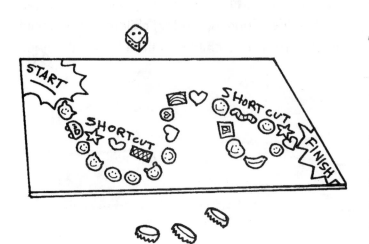

9 Turn shoeboxes on their sides to form bear caves, and place a numeral on the top of each cave. Let your children count out plastic teddy bear counters and put the correct number in each cave.

_____ Trucks	_____ Puppets
_____ Windows	_____ Tables
_____ Balls	_____ Hats

10 Your children can practice counting and writing when they "take inventory" of your room. Make a set of laminated inventory cards. Each card has pictures of five or six classroom items (table, hat, puppet) and a space for recording the number with a wipe-off crayon. Draw the pictures or cut them out of catalogs. Remember to include pictures where the correct answer is zero (hippopotamus, birdhouse, bathtub).

Colors

1 Early in the school year, combine color learning with teaching your children where objects belong in your room. Gather a basket full of learning items of the same color. During large group, have your children take turns returning the items to their proper places. Encourage them to help each other.

2 Play a singing game about colors. Put colored paper circles in a hat or a sock. In turn, have each of your children pull out a circle and show the color. All the children then sing about this color. Make several circles of each color, and make more circles than there are children.

Sung to: "Mary Had a Little Lamb"

Rudy found a color
On a shape that's round.
Rudy found a color,
And red is what he found.

Repeat, substituting the name of one of one of your children for *Rudy,* and the name of the color he or she finds for *red*.

Barbara Backer

3 Match real items to make a color-matching game. Assemble a box of disposable plates, cups, and napkins in various colors. Have your children make sets of matching items.

4 To make a fun color-matching game for the winter months, cut snowman shapes and hats from heavy paper. Draw buttons on each snowman, giving each snowman a different color. Color hats to match the buttons. Have your children match the snowman and hat shapes.

8 Make a book about yellow. Have each of your children contribute a page, drawing what he or she wishes and using mostly yellow in the picture. Label each picture: yellow car, yellow butterfly, yellow ring, and so on. Make a book for each color you study.

9 Have your children help brainstorm a list of possible snacks that match the color you are studying. Red snacks might include spaghetti, pizza, apples, and tomato soup. Select one to serve the next day.

10 Make a color-matching game with index cards and large vinyl-coated paper clips. Using markers that match the paper clip colors, draw a colored stripe on each index card. Make a card to match each clip. To play the game, have your children slide clips onto matching cards.

5 Help your children focus on color with this activity. Cut two 4-inch squares of various fabrics. Have your children match the pairs. (Be careful when cutting plaids or large patterns, so the squares actually match.)

6 Play Color Tag outside. The leader calls out a color, and all your children wearing that color become "It," chasing friends who are not wearing the color. When the leader calls out a new color, the children wearing that color become "It."

7 Let your children discover what happens when they combine colors. Put out a variety of tempera paints, spoons, and jar lids. Have the children mix spoonfuls of color in their jar lids for use at the easel. Begin with two colors, then add more as the year progresses.

Shapes

1 Children learn with their whole bodies. Show them how to use their bodies to make shapes. Arrange three of your children on the floor so their bodies form a triangle. Each child's head touches the feet of another child. Remaining children gather around and count the sides (chests) and corners (heads) of the shape. Later, help children form a square, a circle, or a rectangle.

2 Cut large geometric shapes from appliance boxes. Cut out the center of each shape, yielding a large frame and a smaller solid shape. Place the shapes flat on the floor. Lean the frames against walls and furniture, or suspend them from the ceiling so they just touch the floor. Direct your children to move over, under, around, beside, or through the shapes and frames.

3 Display pictures of shapes. Challenge your children to make similar shapes with pipe cleaners.

4 Arrange paper shapes on the floor and have your children outline them with unit blocks. Remove the paper to reveal the shape's outline. Repeat using pencils, unit cubes, popsicle sticks, buttons, or other objects.

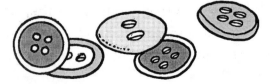

5 Children enjoy making books. Ask your children to make books about triangles. On each page, they can draw or glue a triangle in a different color. Label the pages: red triangle, blue triangle, green triangle. Make similar books for each shape you study.

6 Divide an open file folder into three columns. Across the top draw a triangle, a rectangle, and a circle. Cut index cards in half. On every card draw a picture of an object that includes a basic shape. Have one of your children look at the picture and place it on the folder under the matching shape.

Variation: Instead of index cards, use photographs of real items for this game.

7 Cut geometric shapes from poster-board. Place several pairs of these in a bag. Have your children take turns reaching into the bag and feeling for the shape you request. Vary the game according to each child's abilities: you might ask a child to find a specific shape, such as a square, or two shapes that are the same. With practice, children can tell each other what to pull from the bag.

8 Cut shapes from 4-inch squares of paper, using red for triangles, blue for circles, and yellow for squares (or rectangles). Have your children search the room for shapes: square book, round mixing bowl, triangular coat hanger. Have them put paper shapes near the corresponding items. Write the name of the item on its corresponding precut shape, one item per shape. Help the children graph the shapes. Which one is the most common?

9 Make a set of paper shapes, including at least one example of each shape your children know. Make as many shapes as you have children, plus a few extra. Gather your children in a circle and give each one a paper shape. Then sing the following song, holding up a different paper shape for each verse. Have the children whose shapes match yours hold up their shapes. When every child has held up his or her shape, have the children trade shapes and begin the game again.

Sung to: "The ABC Song"

I have a triangle, look and see.
If you have a triangle, show it to me.

Barbara Backer

10 Encourage family involvement in learning by making a take-home learning game for your children. Cut an assortment of shapes out of different colors of construction paper. Cover each shape with clear self-stick paper for durability. The children can use the shapes to make pictures, or they can sort them according to shape or color. Let each child in turn take the game home for a few days.

Letters

4 Use a black marker and write a different letter on each of 26 index cards. Place five of these in a basket. Add the same letters in wooden, magnetic, and sandpaper letters. Challenge your children to match letters to the letter cards. Change the letters in the basket from time to time.

5 Young children love to hunt for treasure. Give each of your children a letter shape and have him or her find matching letters somewhere in the room. They can look on calendars; on posters; in books, catalogs, and magazines; in phone books; and in many other places.

1 Encourage your children to form letters with modeling dough. Make letter cards by writing one letter on each of 26 index cards. Laminate the cards. Have the children roll modeling dough snakes and arrange the snakes along the letters' outlines.

2 Select four or five plastic letters that have very different shapes, like S, E, R, O, and Y. Place each inside a stretch sock. Make a letter card to match each letter. Have your children feel the plastic letters through the socks and place each sock on the matching letter card. As the children become more confident, add a few more letters and socks. Change letters and letter cards often.

3 Collect a variety of kinds of letters—cardboard, wooden, magnetic, printed on paper, printed on colored index cards, written with white glue on index cards, cut from sandpaper and glued to cardboard, or cut from advertising and glued to index cards.

8 Contact your local school district to find out what style of handwriting (e.g., D'Nealian, Zaner-Bloser, Modern) is taught in kindergarten. Teach your children how to write their name in that style.

9 Write each child's name on an index card, and place the cards in the art center. Children who are ready will copy their names onto their artwork. Place more cards in the language center where the children can copy their own and each other's names.

10 Provide a generous supply of writing materials for your children to use as they experiment with print. Chubby pencils, pens, and crayons are easier for little hands to grip. Wrap rubber bands or masking tape around the ends of pencils for ease in writing.

6 Display a variety of alphabet books in your group's reading area. Read them often, and add new ones regularly. Older children can make their own ABC books. Give each of your children a book with 26 pages and a letter of the alphabet on each page. Over a period of weeks, have the child draw a picture to go with the letter on each page.

7 Have your children use their bodies to form letter shapes on the floor. How many children does it take to make an *I*? An *N*?

Opposites

1 Children learn about opposites by experiencing them. Have a tasting party to taste and identify things that are sweet or sour. Suggestions include graham crackers, apple juice, and jelly; lemon juice, dill pickles, and tart apples.

2 For another experience, have your children stretch up high to become as tall as possible, then stoop very low to become short. Next, tell the children to spread their arms and legs to make themselves very wide, then have them make themselves as narrow as possible.

3 Have your children help you collect items to illustrate large and small. Display the items and compare their sizes.

4 Play Simon Says using opposite concepts: high and low, big and little, near and far.

5 Help your children collect pictures and real items to make a mural of opposites. You might include such items as a new and an old shoelace, a laundry detergent advertisement featuring a clean shirt and a dirty one, pictures of a happy person and a sad one, and pictures of a hot bowl of soup and a cold iced drink.

6 Have your children pose for pictures that illustrate opposites: Justin near and Justin far; the wagon full of children, the wagon empty; the children going up the steps, the same children coming down. Put these pictures side by side in a photo album or a group-made book.

7 Play Follow the Leader, announcing where you are going as you move along: over the balance beam and under the jungle gym, or up the steps and down the slide.

8 Bring in a filled hot water bottle and an ice bag. Pass them around and let your children feel them and discuss them. Make lists of things that are hot and things that are cold.

9 Collect items to illustrate narrow and wide: a regular crayon and a jumbo crayon, or fabric with pinstripes and fabric with wide stripes. Have your children put narrow items together on a long, narrow rectangle of paper and wide items together on a wider paper rectangle.

10 Have your children gather a variety of objects. Now have the children sort them into two categories: hard and soft. Help your children think of other categories by which to sort the items.

Matching

1 Use this matching activity at the beginning of the year to help your children learn where items are in the room. Take photos of items in your room such as a block, a pencil, a crayon, scissors, a doll's shoe, and a paintbrush. During circle time, give a photo to each child. Challenge the children to find the matching items. Have them exchange photos so they put away a different item, learning where it goes.

2 Save decorated cups and napkins from birthday and holiday parties throughout the year. Bring others from fast food restaurants. Place all of these in a box for a matching game.

3 Cut two squares from several patterns of wrapping paper. Glue these on squares of cardboard to make a matching game. To play, spread half the squares on the floor. Place the matching squares in a hat. In turn, let each of your children choose a square from the hat and find its match on the floor.

4 Take pictures of the fronts and backs of familiar items and people: a doll, a chair, a puppet, your program's van, the teacher, a child. Have your children find the matching pairs.

5 Have each of your children (and each teacher) remove one shoe and put it in the middle of the circle. One at a time, give the children a chance to select a shoe and return it to its owner.

6 Make a game that requires your children to match real items to their outlines. On posterboard, trace around several spoons of various sizes, assorted kitchen gadgets, a large paper clip, and other familiar items. Store the gameboard and the items in a box.

7 Videotape your children as they arrive in your classroom, but do not show their heads or faces. Later, show the video and see if the children can identify each other from the body pictures.

8 Ask your children to bring in their baby pictures. Display these and challenge the children to discover the identity of each "mystery baby."

9 Have dolls of different sizes in your room, and provide several sets of clothes for each doll. Children learn reasoning skills as they dress the dolls, matching correct clothes to dolls of different sizes.

10 Can your children match parts of items to the whole item? Display yarn and a crocheted potholder or sweater, a newspaper picture and a section of the newspaper, a telephone book page and a telephone book, a doll shoe and a doll. Challenge the children to think of other possibilities.

Classifying

1 Food activities capture children's attention. Make sorting a part of snacktime. Make a sorting placemat for each of your children by drawing lines to divide a piece of paper into four parts. Glue a circle onto one section and a square, a rectangle, and a triangle onto remaining sections. Cover each with a sheet of plastic wrap before using. Serve each child a handful of crackers in assorted shapes, and let the child sort the crackers on his or her sorting mat.

2 Give each of your children a bottom section of an egg carton and a small plastic bag containing a mixture of raisins, square cereal pieces, O-shaped cereal, dried banana slices, and sunflower seeds. Have the children sort the items into the egg carton cups. Discuss the results. "Juan put all of the dried fruit together. Trina put all of the brown things together." Have them dump everything into the bag and sort items a new way, then invite them to eat their work!

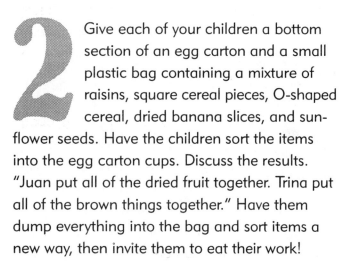

3 Make a "Family Game." Make four columns on a piece of posterboard. Glue a catalog picture of a person at the top of each column—a dad, a mom, a preschool child, and an infant. Make game cards by gluing catalog pictures onto individual index cards. Choose items that would be used by one or more of the people—a lamp, a blender, a crib, a tricycle, a soccer ball, a lawnmower, a purse, etc. Laminate the cards. To play the game, have one of your children give each item to the family member he or she thinks is most appropriate. Accept all responses.

4 Gather empty film canisters (from a photo processing lab) and a variety of scented stickers, four of each scent. Stick each sticker on the lid of a canister. Have your children scratch and sniff the stickers, then put matching canisters together in groups. Surprisingly, children don't sort the stickers by looking at them.

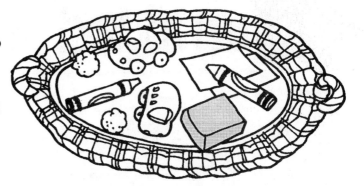

5 Invite a small group of your children to sit in a circle. Roll a ball from one person to another and discuss rolling. Then give each child a basket of small items. Include things that roll (cars, pompons, crayons) and things that do not roll (blocks, magnets, playing cards). Challenge the children to test their items and divide them into two categories: things that roll and things that do not.

6 Play a similar game with magnets. Give each child in your small group a basket containing a magnet and an assortment of items. Include some magnetic items (paper clips, screws) and some nonmagnetic ones (plastic spoons, blocks). Also include items that have magnetic parts (spring-type clothespins, pencils with metal tops.) Give your children time to explore the items and discover that some stick to the magnets. Then have them test each item and sort them into two categories: things that stick to a magnet and things that do not.

7 Make a classifying game based on familiar items. Cut pictures of classroom equipment or housewares from old catalogs. Mount each picture on an index card. Set out the cards and let your children classify the pictures according to their location in the classroom or home.

8 During circle time, call up your children one at a time and sort them into groups. At first tell the children the categories and let them help you decide where each child belongs. Suggested categories: eye color, boy or girl, children wearing blue and children not wearing blue. Next, call the children one at a time and classify them silently. Can the children guess the categories? As the children gain skill, let them take turns directing the classifying.

9 Often children sort items into groups according to someone else's directions: "Put the round ones here and the square ones there." After they have had many experiences doing that, provide your children with opportunities to determine their own categories (classification). Given a container of bottle caps, one child may make groups according to color, another according to size, another according to whether the caps are metal or plastic.

10 From two colors of construction paper, cut out large, medium-sized, and small shapes, including triangles, circles, and squares. Offer these to your children and watch to see if they sort by one, two, or three attributes—color, size, or shape. All responses are acceptable, and new skills will appear over time.

Spatial Relationships

1 Building a small sandwich for snack is a great way to learn about spatial relations. Offer cheese and crackers and sing this song about the finished product.

Sung to: "Down by the Station"

Take a square cracker,
Put it on the bottom,
Cheese in the middle,
And cracker on the top.
Take a big bite now
Of my cracker sandwich.
Crunch, crunch, yum, yum—
Now it's gone!

Barbara Backer

2 Ask your children, "Which is nearer, the trash can or the filing cabinet? The piano or the door?" The children can use different colors of yarn to measure the distances, then compare the lengths of yarn.

Challenge them to think of other ways to measure. They may try walking heel to toe to the object, snapping together unit cubes, or lining up index cards. Try as many as possible. Discuss why some are better than others. When Erica (with big feet) and Alana (with little feet) walk heel to toe to the door, they have different numbers of steps. Why?

3 Movement activities help children become aware of the space occupied by their bodies. They discover that they need more space for running and jumping than for walking and hopping. Help your children discover that hopping is an up-and-down motion, while jumping a distance is a forward motion. Challenge the children to find new ways of moving forward, backward, sideways, and up and down.

4 Take photographs that show spatial relations. Place them in a photo album and label them: "Luis is over Charlie and under Laquita. They are all on the jungle gym"; or "Jenny and Lakisha are beside the tree. Sarita is behind it." Place the photo album in your group's reading area.

5 If one center becomes too crowded with children, ask, "How can we make more room in this center?" Your children may suggest removing items, stacking items, moving shelves and other partitions, moving other furniture, and removing extra children. Discuss how and why different suggestions help or don't help solve the problem. Try all safe suggestions.

6 Have your children make items for a mural about the Three Billy Goats Gruff and the Troll. Label the mural: "The Troll is under the bridge. The biggest goat is on the bridge. Two goats are in the meadow."

7 Set out several small cardboard boxes. How many snap-together unit cubes do your children think these will hold? Have the children work in pairs to fill a box with unit cubes, then remove the cubes and snap them together. Compare the resulting stacks of cubes to compare the volume capacity of the boxes.

8 Provide a variety of large boxes for your children to play with and play in as they explore volume. Ask, "How many children can fit in this box if they are standing? Sitting? How many stuffed animals can fit inside? How many blocks?"

9 Provide a variety of plastic jars and kitchenware containers that each have the same volume capacity but are different shapes. Ask your children if they are the same or if one will hold more. Have a child fill one to the rim with modeling dough. Then have him or her transfer the dough to another container. The children won't immediately understand that the containers hold the same amount. They'll think the modeling dough changed. Store these and similar containers with the modeling dough and keep more in the sand or water table for further experimentation.

10 Provide opportunities for your children to see things from a different perspective. Meet with a small group of children under a table. Discuss what you see from that perspective. Can the children identify their friends by what they see (legs and feet)?

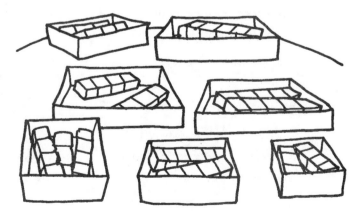

Sequencing and Seriation

1 Ordinal numbers tell the order of things. Your children practice using ordinal numbers when they recite the following fingerplay, pointing to fingers as they go. After they learn the words, five children at a time can act out the rhyme while the remaining children recite it.

The first little frog went hop, hop, hop.
The second little frog said,
"Stop, stop, stop!"
The third little frog stubbed his toe.
The fourth little frog said,
"Oh, oh, oh."
The fifth little frog said,
"I see some flies!"
So the frogs ate dinner
And winked their eyes.
Ribbit! Ribbit! Ribbit! Ribbit! Ribbit!

Barbara Backer

2 Gather four identical cottage cheese (or similar opaque) containers. Fill the first three with varying amounts of salt. Leave the fourth empty. Glue lids on all containers. Have your children lift the containers, compare them, and arrange them in order by weight.

3 Make a sequencing game for each of your children using photographs of the child. Ask his or her parent to send in pictures of the child as an infant, and at ages one, two, and each year up to a current photo. Photocopy the pictures. Mount the copies on cardboard, cut into separate cards, and laminate. Have the child place the photos in order. The children will enjoy playing with one another's cards.

4 Photograph your group's daily activities—circle time, snack, outside play, etc. Show the pictures to your children and let them try to put them in sequence.

5 Take sequential photographs of your children's special projects. For instance, if your children make a mural, take snapshots of the blank paper, the paper with one item on it, with more items, and then the completed mural. Have your children place the photos in order.

6 Play Go Where I Go with your children outdoors. The first child touches an object (the slide). The second child touches the same object plus a second object (the slide, a tree). The third child touches the previous objects in order, plus a third. When a child misses, he or she becomes the first child as the game starts over.

7 Cut three pictures of the same item in three different sizes of items (three shirts, three cars, three W's) from magazines, catalogs, or newspapers. Ask your children to glue the pictures on construction paper from largest to smallest. As the children gain skill, use four or five pictures.

8 Find four identical yogurt containers with opaque lids. Place several nails in one, dried beans in another, salt in the third, and leave the last one empty. Glue the lids on the containers. Have your children shake the containers and place them in order from loudest to quietest. As the children gain skill, add other containers.

9 Children love to sing and they develop auditory memory and sequence skills as they sing songs with many verses. "On Top of Spaghetti" and "I Know an Old Lady" are two examples.

10 Play Move Like Me, Then Add Another with your children. In a circle, the first child makes a motion to music, and all follow along to the count of ten. The second child adds another motion, which the children follow to the count of ten; then they repeat the first motion ten times. Each succeeding child adds another motion until things become too confused. At that point, start again!

Developing Language Skills

Stretching Children's Language

1 Young children's vocabulary grows at an astonishing rate. A child may learn more than a dozen words a day. Learning language is a natural process; children rely on us to teach them the meaning of words. Language is learned through modeling, and we are the models.

2 Be a good language model. Avoid using baby talk. Speak clearly in a normal voice. Use complete sentences and give specific information. If one of your children asks, "Where is Eli?" respond, "Eli is in the snack center," instead of simply pointing and saying, "Over there."

3 As they test new words and sentence structures, young children sometimes make mistakes. Use these opportunities to model correct language. If one of your children says, "I have socks on my foots," restate the child's sentence: "Yes, Daniel, you have socks on your feet."

4 Your responses to your children can also expand their vocabulary. When Danita shows you a doll and says, "I'm playing with the baby doll," respond, "Yes, Danita, you have the biggest baby doll, the one with curly hair."

5 Mysteries capture children's attention. Decorate a large bag as a "Mystery Bag." Fill the bag with common items (crayons, blocks, scissors, etc.). In turn, have each of your children take an item out of the bag, identify the item, and tell what it is used for. Some children will give extended answers: "It's a telephone. When it rings, you pick up this part and say 'Hello.'" Help the child who gives a limited answer. If the child says, "Telephone, rings," respond, "Yes, Cory, it's a telephone and it rings. What do you do when it rings?"

8 Teach your children to count in a foreign language. Ask parents who speak a foreign language for help, or contact the language lab of a local college. A children's librarian can direct you to counting books in Spanish, French, and other languages.

9 Invite visitors to your class to talk about their hobbies and occupations. While they show and tell, your children will learn many new words and concepts.

10 Visit the nonfiction section of the library, and share factual books with your children. They will learn new ideas, concepts, and vocabulary by looking at nonfiction books. Some children especially enjoy pictures of insects and wild animals. Others like pictures of heavy machinery or big trucks and trains. All of these stretch children's language.

6 When a child's language consists of pointing, honor this form of communication. Restate his or her pointing into words. For instance, if one of your children has pointed to the computer in response to your question, "What do you want to play with?" say, "Do you want to play with the computer?" As the child becomes comfortable in your company, encourage him or her to say one or two words.

7 Explain to your children that some people cannot hear spoken language and that they and others use sign language to communicate. Learn simple words in American Sign Language with your children. At first, speak the words as you sign them. Add a new sign each day and practice earlier ones.

Encouraging Oral Expression

1 When planning oral language activities, remember that many children are uncomfortable speaking in front of a group. Offer opportunities for many different types of oral expression, including group singing and chanting, one-on-one conversations, and speaking alone. Be sensitive to your children's feelings—do not pressure the reluctant child to speak.

2 Most children enjoy talking about themselves. Give your children a chance to do this by designating a Star Student each day. This child takes home a star-covered shoebox and a short note inviting him or her to bring the box back to school with three favorite items in it. At circle time, set aside a few minutes for the Star Student to present his or her items.

3 Set up a quiet area where your children can sit with a book and read to a stuffed animal. Make the area large enough for two children who can talk softly, read together, or read to each other.

4 Children are fascinated by the sound of their voices. A megaphone enables them to amplify this sound. Make a megaphone by cutting the large end from a bleach bottle or one-gallon plastic milk jug. Be prepared for loud language!

5 A cassette recorder with a microphone invites oral expression. Place one in your listening area, and language will flourish as your children tell stories, sing songs, and recount their daily experiences on tape.

6 Some children are more verbal than others, and most groups have a chatterbox who seems to never stop talking. Sometimes it is difficult to give this child your full attention. When this happens, help the talkative child find another audience. Children seldom tire of listening to one another and will chatter together at the same time.

7 Children like to imitate adult behavior, including the endless hours we spend on the telephone. Check garage sales for old telephones that your children can use for dramatic play. Include "cordless" models so children can converse indoors and out.

8 Parents often report that their child (who never sings along with the group) is singing all the school songs at home. Remember that some children learn best by watching and listening.

9 Send home words to the songs your children learn at school so parents and children can sing together. Piggyback® songs, sung to familiar melodies, are easy for everyone to learn.

10 Make word games a part of each day. One favorite is to say a word (*hot*) and ask your children to say its opposite (*cold*). Another is to say a word (*tree*) and ask your children to say rhyming words (*bee, see, me*).

Music as a Language Enhancer

3 Movement activities offer opportunities for your children to hear and use new language. Describe their movements to them. As their language skills grow, have them describe one another's movements: "You're moving like swirling leaves. You are on a bucking bronco. I'm flying like a bee. Zzzzz! Sting!"

4 Musical games offer opportunities to expand vocabulary. Children learn and practice using names of body parts when they play Hokey-Pokey and Looby Loo. Don't worry about right and left when they play. Sing, "I put one hand in...," then, "I put the other hand in...." This places the emphasis on learning body parts. Let each of your children choose a body part to sing about in turn. Encourage unusual answers like lip, elbow, or hip. The more parts the children name, the more they will learn.

5 Children love to make and play rhythm instruments. Encourage your children to use language to describe each instrument's sound.

1 It's easy to learn words when they are put to music, as anyone who's been unable to forget a commercial jingle knows. Songs expose children to the rhythm, tone, and pitch of language.

2 Children need to know their address and telephone number in case of an emergency. Help your children learn this kind of rote information through song. A child who knows the following tune will easily remember his or her telephone number.

Sung to: "The ABC Song"

Yes, I know my phone number,
555-1212.
555-1212,
555-1212.
Yes, I know my phone number,
555-1212.

Barbara Backer

8 When selecting multicultural music for your children, include songs from different regions of the United States as well as music from other countries. For instance, songs from the Southwest represent another culture to children in New England.

9 Add to your music collection at no cost by borrowing songbooks, cassettes, and CDs from the public library.

10 If you don't read music, ask a friend who does to tape-record the melody lines of songs. Use the tape to learn the songs, then put it in the listening area so your children can listen and sing along.

6 At group time, tape record your children singing a new or favorite group song. Write the song on a chart. Play the tape and point to the chart as the children listen to and sing along with the tape. Place the tape and the chart in the listening area, where the children can listen, sing along, and "read" the song all at the same time.

7 Help your children understand that both music and language are ways of expressing feelings and images. Play instrumental music for the children and encourage them to use words to describe it. How does the music make them feel? Happy? Sad?

Flannelboard Tips

3 To make flannelboard characters, lay a sheet of thin Pellon interfacing (from a fabric store) over a coloring-book figure. Trace the lines lightly with pencil. Cut out the figure and color it with permanent markers. (The color takes a few hours to dry; until then, it will rub off on hands and clothing.)

4 Tired of tracing and cutting felt shapes for your flannelboard? Use a magnet-board instead. Cover a nonaluminum baking sheet with solid color self-stick paper. Cut shapes, numerals, letters, or story characters from old books or magazines, and mount them on heavy paper. Laminate these, then attach a piece of adhesive-backed magnetic strip (available at hardware stores) to the back of each.

1 Pictures help young children understand the connection between words and the things they represent. For this reason, flannelboard activities are a wonderful way to present rhymes, stories, and songs. Include a flannelboard in your language center, and you'll find many uses for it.

2 For large, inexpensive flannelboards, look for discarded table protection pads at garage sales. The bottom surface is brushed felt—perfect for a flannelboard. Unfold the pad for a huge display surface, or cut the pad apart at each fold for smaller individual boards. Rectangular pads can be set on end and used as flannelboard room dividers.

5 Cover the top half of a magnetboard with blue self-stick paper and the bottom half with green to make a background of land and sky for your magnetboard characters.

6 Following from left to right and top to bottom is a reading readiness skill that your children learn through example. Always display and point out flannelboard items from left to right and from top to bottom.

7 Flannelboard activities also help your children understand story sequence and ordinal numbers. As you tell stories on the flannelboard, point out what comes first, second, and third.

8 Recycle worn-out picture books by cutting out the pictures of the story's characters and using them on a flannelboard. Glue them onto stiff paper, laminate them, then glue a piece of sandpaper to the back. Let your children tell the stories in their own way.

9 Children enjoy seeing real people represented in learning activities. Use photos of your children on a magnetboard, or cut and mount multicultural pictures from magazines to use with the flannelboard.

10 Use flannelboard characters to help your children learn and remember the verses in cumulative songs such as "I Know an Old Lady." As you sing the song, point to each character as it is mentioned. Leave the figures on the flannelboard so the children can use them to sing the song on their own.

Puppets

5 Making puppets is only half the fun. Encourage your children to teach their puppets to recite rhymes and sing songs.

6 To make quick, inexpensive puppets, you can use precut paper shapes (available from parent-teacher stores). Staple a shape to a tongue depressor or craft stick and you have an instant stick puppet.

1 Puppets invite interaction. Try using puppets to comfort your children when they are hurt or frightened. Sometimes a child will respond better to a puppet than to a person, especially if the puppet is soft and cuddly.

2 Because they capture children's attention, puppets are a great way to communicate important information. Puppets can teach your children telephone etiquette, safety tips, and many other things.

3 Shy children often find it easier to express themselves when they are wearing a hand puppet. Have puppets available at circle time and throughout the day for children who need them.

4 Children like to make their own puppets. Have your children use permanent felt tip markers to draw facial features on wooden or plastic spoons. Cut a circle of fabric for clothing. Insert the spoon's handle in a slit you cut in the circle's center. Use rubber bands to attach the costume to the spoon.

9 Many children are afraid of having a mask tied over their face. Face puppets are a less threatening alternative. Have each of your children create a face on a small paper plate using felt tip markers or construction paper and glue. Attach a craft stick handle and have the child hold the plate in front of his or her face to use the mask.

7 For a quick-and-easy finger puppet, attach a sticker to your fingertip. Look for stickers that relate to your children's favorite rhymes, songs, and stories.

8 The simplest throwaways make great puppets. Use felt tip markers or construction paper and glue to decorate a toilet tissue tube. If desired, add arms made from chenille stems or construction paper strips. Insert your fingers in the tube's bottom to make the puppet move.

10 Stage a puppet show with your children. Turn a table on its side to make an impromptu puppet theater. Have the children crouch behind the table to perform. To make a permanent puppet theater, remove the back and internal parts from a discarded console TV. When your children climb inside, their puppets appear to perform on television.

Using Books

1 One of our most important jobs as teachers is to help children fall help-lessly in love with books. A person who loves to read will be a lifelong learner. Surround your children with books of all shapes and sizes, and read, read, read!

2 When children are authors, their interest in books grows. As a group, make a book for your book corner. You might start by taking a photograph of each of your children. Photocopy each photo on a separate sheet of paper and ask each child to dictate a few words about his or her photo. Write the child's exact words on the page to reinforce the connection between written and spoken language. Cover each page with clear self-stick paper, and add your own page before binding the pages together.

3 Encourage reading at home by making group books that your children can share with their families. Take pictures of the children engaged in learning activities, celebrating special days, and going on outings. With the children's help, mount these in a photo album. Add captions, if desired. Let each child take the album home for a few days. Make many albums throughout the year.

4 At story time, ask your children what book they want you to read. Encourage them to tell you more and more about the book as you pretend you don't remember the story.

5 Once in a while, introduce a new book to your children by showing them the illustrations. Ask the children to describe what is happening in each picture. Encourage them to tell a story based on the illustrations. Then read the words. Is the author's story similar or different?

6 As children hear more stories, they begin to understand that each has a beginning, a middle, and an end. Guided questions can help your children make sense of the stories they hear. When you finish a story, ask the children to recall the order of events: What did the Little Red Hen do first? What happened next? What was the last thing that happened in the story?

7 Some children never experience the pleasure of being read to individually. Consider recruiting adult volunteers to read to your children one-on-one. (Many retirees delight in spending quiet time with little ones.) Also arrange for your group to share books with older or younger children from other classrooms.

8 At the library, find books that have pictures of great works of art. Show pictures to your children and encourage them to discuss what they see. Still lifes allow the children to talk about fruits, vegetables, flowers, and more. Landscapes encourage discussion of outdoor activities, weather, and geographic terrain. Children love to look at portraits from long ago and talk about the clothing and hair styles.

9 Stimulate discussion by asking open-ended questions after you read a story. Ask questions such as these: "What do you think Corduroy was thinking when he saw Lisa and her mother shopping in the store? Where do you think Harry will go next time he leaves home?" Accept all answers.

10 Make books a part of group celebrations. For each child's birthday, ask his or her family to donate a paperback book to your classroom library. Invite the child's family to come in and share the book with your group.

Modeling Reading

3 Make modeling dough with your children. Read the recipe aloud to them from your recipe file, then let them watch as you write a picture recipe on chart paper. Read the completed picture recipe with the children, and read it again, step by step, as you and the children follow the directions and make the modeling dough.

4 Children are fascinated by the newspaper because it seems to be for adults only. Read to your group from the newspaper every day. Post picture stories on the bulletin board.

5 Children are often asked to deliver notes between school and home. Include your children in this communication by reading notes aloud to the group before they are carried home. When a child brings you a note from home, if the message is appropriate for sharing, read the note to the child.

1 Example is the best teacher, so be certain that your children see you and others reading often, both for information and for pleasure. Help the children discover how reading and writing are related. Send notes back and forth to other teachers: "May we borrow your glue? Do you have a book about bears?" When you receive a note, read it aloud.

2 Children and pizza seem to go together. Plan together to order pizza for your group's lunch or snack. Show your children the menu from a pizza parlor. Read the list of ingredients aloud. Show them the telephone number on the menu and have them watch and listen as you call to order the pizza. Have it delivered directly to your room. Enjoy!

9 Everybody enjoys receiving mail. Ask traveling parents to send postcards or letters to your group. Read these aloud to your children and display them where the children can handle and "read" them.

10 Take advantage of children's interest in food. If your program serves lunch, post the weekly lunch menu in your room. Every morning, read the menu for that day's lunch, and at the end of one day read the menu for the next. See if your children can remember the menu the following day. Make picture menus for younger children.

6 You can model reading as your group prepares for a field trip. Before an outing to a museum or other tourist attraction, bring in brochures about the place. Let your children explore these materials, then have them listen as you read a few of the highlights. Cut pictures from the brochures. Give one picture to each child to carry on the trip. As you tour, have the children look for the real item that matches the one on their picture.

7 When you go on your field trip, ask adults at the destination to show you some of the materials they read on the job. For instance, firefighters read maps and checklists, museum curators read reports, and grocery store clerks read labels.

8 Invite people to come in and read to your children. Include people they admire—parents or grandparents, a police officer, a veterinarian, even the host of a local children's television program.

Finding Words Everywhere

1 Words are all around us—on calendars, in newspapers and telephone books, on advertising, and on signs. Take advantage of children's interest in this environmental print. One simple way is to take photos of traffic signs. Make duplicates of each photo. Use these as a matching game.

2 Place a discarded telephone book with a telephone in the dramatic play center. Have your children look for familiar logos in the Yellow Pages and tell what each logo stands for.

3 Before the age of three, most children can identify the logos and signs of fast-food restaurants. Collect placemats, cups, wrapped straws, and other items from fast-food restaurants. Children will recognize and "read" the logos and can match items from the same restaurant. Place the items in the dramatic play center so your children can create their own restaurant.

4 Show your children the exit signs in your facility. Explain what an exit is. Can they find other exit signs when you go on field trips?

5 Take photos of familiar neighborhood signs: street signs, restaurant and store logos, and the sign in front of your facility. Put these in photo albums for your children to "read."

6 Help your children make sense of the calendar. Make word cards for the days of the week. Put them on a table along with several calendars. Challenge the children to look for words on the calendars that match those on the cards. Discuss the words and their order on the calendar.

7 Children love videos and can identify the tapes by looking at the boxes. Select several favorites. Make two photocopies of each box and mount each copy on cardboard to make a matching game.

8 Grocery ads are especially useful because they include words and pictures. Show the grocery ads from the newspaper. Make a game where your children match real items to newspaper advertisements.

9 Children can match words by shape long before they can read them. Find two identical grocery ads. Cut up one to make word cards using words from the ad. Spread the other ad on the table. Have your children choose a card and try to find the matching word in the ad. Discuss the words and the purpose of the ad. Make similar cards from the ad's numerals.

10 Surround your children with environmental print. Place empty food packages in the dramatic play center. Bring in programs from sporting events and concerts, airline tickets, junk mail, dictionaries, coupons, golf score cards, maps, and more.

Socialization

1 Games help children learn social skills. Remind your children about using *please* and *thank you* while they play the following circle game. Give an item (any object from your room will work) to one of your children. Then sing the following song.

Sung to: "Frère Jacques"

First child: May I have that?
 May I have that?
Second child: Yes, you may.
 Yes, you may.
(Second child hands object to first child.)
First child: Thank you very much.
 Thank you very much.
Second child: You are welcome.
 You are welcome.
(First child turns to third child and the game continues.)

2 Some telephone companies have real "learning" telephones to lend to teachers. These are connected to each other and really ring when one child telephones another. During circle time, discuss telephone manners and act out phone calls with your children. Then make the phones available for their play during center time. If these phones aren't available, use discarded phones purchased at garage sales. They won't be connected electronically, but the children can sit close together to hear each other.

3 Play "What Do You Say, What Do You Do?" to help your children learn what to say in different situations at school. Ask them to think of an appropriate response for situations such as these: someone steps on your toe; you step on someone's toe; someone has the crayon you want to use.

4 The "What Do You Say, What Do You Do?" game can also help your children learn what to say and do in situations away from school. For instance, what do you say or do when you want to watch cartoons but your sister is watching her favorite program on TV? When you spill a glass of milk?

5 Plan activities where your children work together in pairs. Pair children who seldom play together so they can learn social skills with a new person. Put each pair on a beach towel with a floor puzzle to work together. Or give each pair a pile of modeling dough or a few interlocking construction pieces.

6 In group games such as "The Farmer In the Dell," where one child chooses the next child, give the choosers a bit of direction to ensure that all of your children have an equal number of turns. Say, "When you choose, choose someone with a brown belt," stating a characteristic of a child who has not yet been chosen. Avoid singling out the unchosen children by name. Saying, "Choose someone who is taller than Carey," or, "Choose the child with the longest hair," narrows the choices in a positive direction and challenges the chooser's problem-solving skills as well.

7 Set up your room to promote socialization. When two easels are side by side, your children can discuss their paintings. Have enough toys for everyone and provide duplicates of popular toys to prevent squabbles over who gets to use something. Place several baby dolls in the dramatic play center to prevent arguments over parenthood. Make learning centers as large as possible to admit everyone who wants to play.

8 Children are just learning to use language. It's easier for them to hit, scream, or cry when they are frustrated or feel angry with each other. At these times, help your children put their feelings into words. Say, "You are feeling angry because you want to play with that truck. Tell Sarita what you want." Then say to Sarita, "What do you want to tell Yoni?" In time, the children will settle more and more squabbles with language.

9 Songs such as the following one are a reminder of the value of friendships. Substitute the names of your children for those in the song, and repeat the song until everyone's name has been used.

Sung to: "She'll Be Coming Round the Mountain"

Oh, I like to go to school
    with all my friends.
Oh, I like to go to school
    with all my friends.
There are Tony, Luis, and Eric,
And Keisha, Garth, and Emily,
Oh, I like to go to school
    with all my friends.

Barbara Backer

10 Be a model for using gentle language to settle disputes. Say, "I know you want to ride the tricycle, but screaming won't get you a turn. Come stand by me. I'll rub your back while you wait." Or, "I won't let you kick Carlo, and I won't let him kick you, either. We don't kick at school."

Rhyme and Repetition

1 "Read it again. Can we sing it again?" These words tell us that children love to hear the same stories and sing favorite songs again and again. Children learn through meaningful repetition, so honor their wishes, even if you are tired of the old standards. Offer new songs, stories, and rhymes, and repeat them, too, until they become favorites.

2 The library is a good place to check out many books of poetry for children. You can find poems to enhance every unit of study. Read many different kinds of poems to your children. Read a poem a day for the beauty of the language and the rhyme.

3 Many of today's young ones grow up knowing no nursery rhymes. Introduce your children to these classics and watch their auditory memory and rhyming skills grow. Recite nursery rhymes during circle time or outside as you push a child on the swing. The children will chant with you while stirring up a snack or cleaning up the room. Let the children act out selected nursery rhymes as a group. Half the group can be Miss Muffet and half can be the spider.

4 To help your children learn rhymes, recite the rhyme one or two times. Recite it again, but leave off the last word of each line, pausing to allow the children to fill in the empty space. Now leave off two or three words. Soon the children will be reciting the entire rhyme with you.

5 When you add movement to rhymes, children seem to learn them more quickly. After a few repetitions, your children will know the entire piece. Add motions to the following rhyme.

My hands go clap, my feet go tap,
I bow and touch the ground.
I stretch up high, up toward the sky;
My hands go round and round.
My arms go down, I turn around
And stamp three times, you see.
I sit right down upon the ground,
As quiet as can be.

Barbara Backer

6 Teach your children jump rope rhymes from your childhood. (If your memory is a bit foggy, a librarian can direct you to books of these and other street rhymes.) They are fun to chant outdoors or in. Can the children think up movements to go with the steady beat?

7 Children enjoy playing this matching game that relies on their knowledge of rhymes. Gather items for a Rhyming Box and put it in the language center. Your children can help by bringing items from home. Suggested items: doll's sock, lock; toy tree, key; toy house, toy mouse. Have the children spread out the items and put rhyming ones together. Ask one child to check another's efforts, and the second child will be learning, too.

8 Children learn from each other when they play group games. Make a small poster with a dozen or more pictures of items whose names have several rhyming words: for instance, *ants*, *pig*, *box*, *hat*, *cat*, and *socks*. Show the poster and ask your children, "Who can find a picture that rhymes with *mat*? Who can find a picture that rhymes with *blocks*?" You can make up nonsense words, too: "Who can find a picture that rhymes with *yake*? With *blar*?" The children respond with words, or shy children might respond by pointing to the matching picture.

9 Most children's songs are full of rhyming words. Expose your children to plenty of songs so they can hear the words' similar sounds. Children who know "Twinkle, Twinkle, Little Star" already know a rhyming word for *star* and another for *sky*.

10 Repetitive stories help children learn language patterns. When you tell these stories to your children, encourage them to chant along with the Billy Goats and the Troll, to help the Gingerbread Boy chant as he speaks to each animal, and to help Maurice Sendak's Pierre say, "I don't care."

Developing Motor Skills

Small Muscle Coordination

1 Fingerplays build muscle coordination and strength in little fingers. Fingers learn to move one at a time while you sing and illustrate "Where Is Thumbkin?" It's fun to draw a face on each finger with a washable pen before singing.

2 The index finger, middle finger, and thumb are used for holding and guiding pencils and pens. Children develop practice using these fingers when they squeeze and release spring-type clothespins in this game. Divide a cardboard pizza round into eight or more wedges. Color the wedges with markers. Color wooden clothespins to match each wedge. Have your children pinch clothespins to place them on the rim of the matching-colored section.

3 Using tweezers is also a good finger exercise. Make another game by putting various-sized pompons into a shallow margarine tub. Provide tweezers and another tub. Have your children use tweezers to move the pompons from one container to the other.

4 Provide a container of colored, vinyl-coated paper clips, large and small. Children will automatically hook them together, sometimes practicing classifying or patterning skills while they build coordination.

5 Add index cards to the previous activity. Offer no suggestions on the cards' use. Let your children's creative instincts lead them.

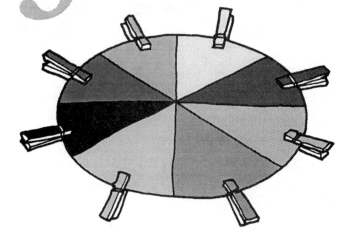

6 Cooking activities provide opportunities to use small muscles. Make a fruit salad using melon balls that your children scoop from ripe melons. Spread butter, peanut butter, or soft cream cheese on crackers.

7 Exercise small muscles in the feet and toes. Ask your children to remove their shoes and socks. Then have them roll paper into small balls to pick up with their toes. Try picking up pencils or small toys, too.

8 Put pegs and pegboards in your dramatic play center. Children will use them to create birthday cakes and other delicacies. Encourage your children to weave lengths of yarn or thin strips of fabric around and through the pegs in their creations.

9 To help your children develop hand-eye coordination and hammering skills, tightly fill a large plastic margarine tub with modeling clay. Provide a wooden hammer and golf tees for children to hammer into the clay.

10 Put spring-type metal clips at the easels. Show your children how to get their own paper, clip it to the easel, then hang the finished painting on a drying line. They'll learn independence while they gain small muscle coordination.

Music and Movement

1 Dancing with streamers elongates the body's motion and provides a gentle stretch to muscles. Make streamer wands by cutting 3-foot-long strips from crepe paper. Fold the strips in half. Flatten one end of a paper towel tube. Insert the folded edge of the streamer into the flattened end of the tube, then staple it closed.

2 Have your children hold streamer wands while they move creatively to gentle, swaying music. Ask them to move the wand high, low, in front of, beside, and behind the body. Have children observe how their movements change when they move to country, rock, or marching rhythms. Move to music from different cultures.

3 Children like glittery, shimmering streamers. Create them by folding a handful of tinsel icicles in half. Wrap tightly at the fold with tape to make handles. Eighteen-inch lengths of tinsel garlands make glittery streamers, too.

4 Obtain large scarves at garage sales. Flatten one against a child's back, then tie the top two corners loosely around the child's neck to form a regal robe. Add a construction paper crown, and have your children march to processional music. Remove the crown and the children become superheroes, soaring to lilting music. Tie bandannas around their necks and watch the children ride imaginary horses to galloping music.

5 Children enjoy moving like animals. Sing the following song and move as the song directs.

Sung to: "Turkey in the Straw"

Oh, you move your arms,
Then your legs move, too.
And you move your body
Like the turkeys do.
Oh, you waddle and you waddle
And you waddle some more.
Then you gobble and you gobble,
As you move around the floor.

Gobble, gobble, gobble;
Gobble, gobble, gobble, gobble.
Gobble, gobble, gobble;
Gobble, gobble, gobble, gobble.
Oh, you waddle and you waddle
And you waddle some more.
Then you gobble and you gobble,
As you move around the floor.

Barbara Backer

6 Use a portable stereo to take music outside. Take advantage of the extra space for marching, hopping, skipping, running, and dancing.

7 Have your children use their bodies to make sounds to accompany music both indoors and out. Clapping hands, tapping toes, and stomping feet are a beginning. What sounds can they make while walking through dried leaves? While sliding their feet through acorns or seashells?

8 Pair up your children for a cooperative movement activity. Have one child move to slow music while the other follows directions to move streamers over, under, beside, behind, around, or in front of his or her partner.

9 Show your children that skipping is a step-then-hop-on-one-foot movement. Step-hop, change feet; step-hop on the other foot, change feet. Do this in slow motion while singing this song, and invite the children to join in. Gradually increase speed. When the children gain skill and confidence, skip to the following song.

Sung to: "Yankee Doodle"

Step and hop and step and hop,
Step and hop and step and hop,
Step and hop and step and hop,
That's the way to skip.

Barbara Backer

10 End movement time with a relaxing activity. After your children pretend they are frisky puppies jumping to catch butterflies and barking at cats, have them yawn, stretch their puppy backs, then plop down on the floor. Slowly, they curl up, pulling back paws under their bodies. Finally, have them place puppy heads on their front paws, and rest.

Dressing Skills

1 Encourage parents to dress children in easy-to-manage clothing. Children are more likely to attempt to dress themselves when their clothing is easy to put on and take off. Avoid belts, pants with stiff snaps, and overalls with hard-to-open snaps and buttons. Best choices are elastic-waist pants and pullover knit shirts.

2 For stubborn zippers and reluctant snaps—usually found on jeans—rub the metal zipper with a pencil point. (The graphite lubricates the metal.) For reluctant snaps, stick the pencil point into the metal snap's top and run it round and round. This must be repeated after each washing.

3 For ease in putting on shoes, tell a child that the shoe is a monster. The opening is its mouth; the shoe's tongue is the monster's tongue. The monster must open its mouth very wide and lift its tongue to get the foot in. Then it puts down its tongue and (as laces are pulled tight) closes its teeth.

4 Children can put on their jackets independently. Lay the jacket on its back on the floor. Spread open the front. Have the child lie down on top of the jacket, slip his or her arms into the jacket's arms, and stand up.

5 Show your children how buttons work—by sliding them sideways through the buttonhole. Help them see that tugging on a garment or using a "ripping" motion won't work. Slightly stretch the buttonholes of clothes in the dramatic play center to make them easier to button.

6 In the dramatic play center, provide dolls of various sizes and an assortment of clothing for each one. Include clothes that have a variety of fasteners, including large and small snaps, large hook-and-eye closings, zippers, and Velcro. On "dress-up" garments, replace tiny snaps or tiny hooks and eyes with larger ones.

7 Begin to teach zipping when children first wear cool-weather jackets that have big zippers. Show your children, one at a time, how to bring the zipper's pull to the bottom, flatten the pull, and hold it closed. Show them the long, thin opening this creates, and the long, thin end of the zipper's other side that will slide into this opening. Demonstrate sliding one side into the other, then show how to pull up on the zipper's pull to zip up the jacket.

8 Show your children that unzipping is the reverse of zipping—it involves sliding the pull to the bottom of the zipper's track. Pulling both sides of the jacket apart sideways will often break a zipper, but it will never unzip it.

9 Positioning fingers to put on mittens is easier when children sing this song.

Sung to: "The Farmer in the Dell"

My fingers stand up straight.
My thumb moves away.
I put on my mittens,
And I go outside to play.

Barbara Backer

10 Opening and closing pocketbooks, backpacks, suitcases, briefcases, coin purses, lunchboxes, and other containers gives children practice with zippers, snaps, buttons, buckles, and more. Include these items in the dramatic play center.

Cutting Skills

1 Cutting requires finger strength and coordination. The movements to the following song develop both.

Sung to: "Jimmy Crack Corn"

Open wide, squeeze them tight.
Open wide, squeeze them tight.
Open wide, squeeze them tight—
Move your fingers right.

Barbara Backer

2 Fingers open and the thumb pulls away as you cut. Help children practice this motion without scissors on their hands while they sing the following song.

Sung to: "Old MacDonald Had a Farm"

Watch my fingers open, shut;
That's the way I cut.

Barbara Backer

Have your children continue "cutting" in time to the song, this time with real scissors (but without paper).

3 Once your children have mastered the cutting motion, help them make their first cuts on paper. As a child opens and closes the scissors, glide a piece of paper between the blades so that he or she is snipping "fringe" along the paper's edge. When the child is accustomed to the feel of scissors on paper, he or she is ready to cut paper in half. Select a sheet of heavy paper (an index card works well) and guide it through the child's scissors as he or she cuts through the middle. Finally, demonstrate how to hold the scissors in one hand and the paper in the other. To help your children remember to move the paper through the scissors (instead of vice versa), ask them to imagine that their cutting arms are anchored to the table with sticky glue.

4 Have your children practice cutting modeling dough to build strength and skill. Designate several pair of scissors just for use with modeling dough. Start by cutting skinny snakes, then thicker ones. Have your children use a rolling pin to flatten pieces of dough. They can cut these with scissors, too. Providing tongue depressors or plastic knives gives another kind of cutting practice.

5 Give beginners long strips of ½-inch-wide paper to snip. Next, give them similar strips that have thick lines drawn across them. Have your children practice cutting "on the line." Gradually give wider strips of paper, and eventually draw wavy lines as cutting guides. Finally, draw zigzags and show the children how to stop cutting and turn the paper in the scissors before continuing.

6 Young ones enjoy cutting paper into tiny scraps. Encourage this practice by providing special envelopes or small bags to collect the scraps in and carry them home. Or save the scraps for collage projects.

7 Avoid using thin, lightweight paper, which is difficult for beginners to cut. Use index cards, or ask printing shops to donate scraps of card tag and other heavy stock for practice.

8 Holidays are great times for scissors practice. Give your children the toy and gift ads from magazines and newspapers. They'll cut happily for long periods of time as they select what they would like to receive and what they would like to give to others.

9 Children practice cutting when they use scissors to create Tiger Stripe snacks. (Sanitize scissors beforehand by soaking them in a solution of one part chlorine bleach to ten parts water.) Have each child toast a slice of whole wheat bread. Let him or her cut across a slice of cheese to make four or more strips and lay these on the bread with a bit of the brown bread showing through. Put the sandwich under the broiler just until the cheese begins to melt. Delicious!

10 Children can cut safely with plastic serrated knives. Wrap a rubber band around the handle for a secure grip. Let your children make individual fruit salads. Give each child small pieces of apple and pear, one-fourth of a banana, and a few raisins on a piece of waxed paper. Have the children cut the fruit into bite-size pieces and put the salad in a paper cup. Let them drizzle on orange juice for a zesty dressing, and snack is served.

Weaving, Braiding, and Sewing Skills

1 For first attempts at weaving, give each child a plastic berry basket and a handful of colored pipe cleaners. Explain that weaving is an in-and-out process, and show your children how to weave the pipe cleaners in and out of the basket holes. When they are finished, help them add pipe cleaner handles. No matter how many holes they skip or what direction they go, the results are colorful and useful. Encourage all efforts.

2 Weaving is easier when the materials are large. Have your children decorate a chainlink fence by weaving long strips of colorful fabric in and out of the fence holes. Weave in natural materials like sticks and tall grasses. Use yarn to tie on feathers, leaves, and blossoms. Make this a long-term project. A few snips with scissors make cleanup fast and easy.

3 Give each child a 4-inch square of burlap to examine. Show your children how to unravel the fabric by pulling the strands one at a time. Give each child a small plastic bag to carry home the resulting threads.

4 Simplify braiding by twisting together the ends of three differently colored pipe cleaners. Fasten this end to a fixed object, such as a nail in a board. Show your children the process of alternating from side to side, always putting the outside color over the middle one. These braids make colorful bracelets and other accessories.

5 Make sewing cards by cutting simple shapes from a 9-by-12-inch piece of posterboard. Make holes along the edge, 1 inch apart, with a hole punch. Tie a 6-foot piece of yarn to one of the holes. Dip the other end of the yarn in glue and let it dry to form a "needle." Show your children how to sew in and out or around and around the edge.

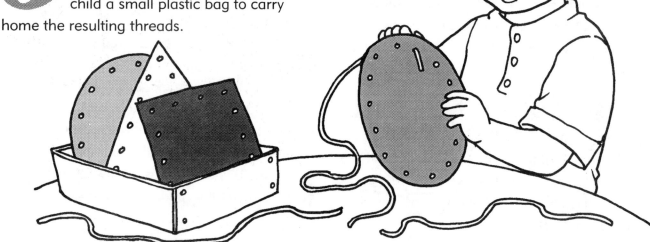

9 Show your children how to sew two items together. With a stapler, tack two sheets of paper together. Have the children punch holes along three edges of the paper. Attach yarn to the first hole and attach a twist tie needle (as in tip 6). Have each child make a pouch by sewing around the three sides. He or she can use the pouch to carry home artwork.

10 Attach yarn pieces to citrus net bags. Thread yarn ends into large plastic needles. Have your children sew in and out of the bags' holes. Then have them pull out their stitches. Seeing the sewing process reversed increases thinking skills.

6 To make a quick and easy "needle" for sewing card projects, tie the end of the yarn around the center of a twist tie. Fold the twist tie in half so the ends meet, then twist the ends tightly together.

7 Buy large plastic needles with big eyes at craft or needlework shops. Thread these with yarn. Cut 12-inch squares of burlap and run a line of glue around the edges to prevent raveling. Buy large, two-hole buttons at craft or fabric stores, or cut large buttons from posterboard. Show your children how to sew on the buttons, then let them practice.

8 Purchase plastic needlework canvas at craft stores. Trace a shape or simple picture onto it with markers. Thread a large plastic needle with yarn for your children to use to stitch in and out of holes along the lines.

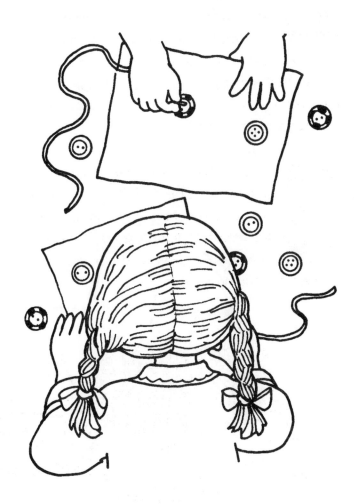

Outdoor Play

1 Outdoor play provides opportunities for children to develop physical fitness and relieve stress. Enjoy a brisk daily walk with your children before or after playtime. Use outdoor space to run, gallop, hop, and jump.

2 Children love to fall down, then get up—again and again. Sing the following song as your children hold hands and move around in a circle. Fall down on the final BOOM!

Sung to: "Here We Go Looby Loo"

Here we go round and round,
Singing a merry tune.
Here we go round and round,
Then we all fall down—BOOM!

Barbara Backer

3 Headbands enhance children's creative motor play outdoors. Children wearing frog headbands will hop across imaginary ponds, while children wearing cat ears stalk imaginary mice. Other ideas include rabbit ears, mouse ears, bear ears, and police officers' or fire fighters' insignias.

4 Have your children set up a variety of pathways leading from one piece of equipment to another. They will enjoy stepping sideways on rope paths, walking backward between lines of empty milk cartons, and hopping between rows of pine cones. Encourage them to make pathways of rocks, leaves, or shells and decide how to move through them.

5 Give your children opportunities to rake leaves, straw, sand, and other natural materials. Purchase child-size rakes or cut the handles of standard-size tools to the proper height for children. Children also enjoy sweeping outside walkways and steps with small brooms.

6 Place a Hula Hoop on the ground. Children can use it as a target for throwing. Provide beanbags or bottle caps, or challenge your children to use natural materials like pine cones or seed pods.

7 Add music to your outdoor play. Bring a portable stereo outside. With no introduction, play music from superhero movies and watch children "fly" around the yard. Play marches, and see how the movement and play changes. Repeat this regularly, introducing waltzes, polkas, minuets, and music from many lands.

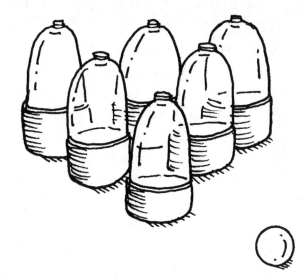

8 Arrange plastic soda bottles in a triangle like bowling pins. Have your children take turns knocking them down with a ball or beanbags. Let the children set up the bottles in any pattern they wish and make up their own rules about where to stand to roll the ball or throw the beanbags. Don't worry about keeping score. The fun comes from actively playing.

9 Children like to draw on pavement with chalk, and they're strengthening both large and small muscles while they bend to draw. Have them draw a path of stepping stones to hop on or a roadway to ride through on tricycles.

10 Sunny days are perfect for building hand-eye coordination while fishing. Put a few inches of water in a wading pool. Cut small fish shapes from plastic bottles. Put a paper clip on each fish's nose. Hang a magnet on a string from the end of a dowel to make a fishing pole. Put the fish in the pool, give your children fishing poles, and let them catch their "limit."

Sifting and Digging Fun

1 Children like to use real equipment. Put trowels, spades, and other gardening tools in the sandbox. Provide child-size spades, hoes, and cultivators, or buy small adult versions and cut the handles down to fit children. Add a small wheelbarrow or cart for moving dirt. Help your children assume the responsibility of cleaning and drying tools at the end of each play period to protect them from rust.

2 To promote digging, paint rocks or seashells with gold spray paint, then bury them in the sand. At the end of outdoor time, encourage children to bury them again for the next group to discover. Let children suggest other treasures to bury, such as milk bottle tops, seed pods, and pine cones.

3 Plastic bottles with handles can be cut into scoops and diggers. Leave bottle caps on. Cut off the bottom end of various-size soda bottles (caps removed) to make funnels.

4 For a summertime treat, have your children put on bathing suits at school, then celebrate "Mud Day." Let them help you add water to a wading pool with dirt in it, then stir and stir to produce mud. Can they tell you what muscles they are using while squeezing, digging, and walking in mud?

5 To reduce the incidence of sand in your children's eyes, show them how thrown sand is carried by the wind. Explain that even though they don't throw sand at others, the wind can carry it into playmates' eyes and mouths. When children understand this, they are less likely to throw sand in the air.

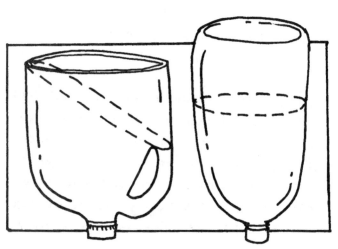

6 Set out a variety of sieves, strainers, berry baskets, colanders, and sifters for your children to use. Have the children compare the merits and disadvantages of each.

7 Challenge your children to make sifters for the sandbox. Provide pie plates, pieces of paper and cardboard, plastic bottles, plastic jar lids, paper punches, hammers and nails (if children are skilled with them), and other items. Encourage all efforts and let the children evaluate the results. Which work best? Which are the most durable?

8 Allow your children to bring cars, trucks, blocks, multiethnic figures, plastic animals, pots, pans, cooking utensils, and other "indoor" items to the sand area. Be certain the children understand it is their responsibility to wash or brush off these items before bringing them back inside.

9 Singing always makes the work go smoother, whether digging or sifting.

Sung to: "Row, Row, Row Your Boat"

Dig, dig, dig the sand,
Dig a hole that's deep.
My shovel helps me move the sand
And push it in a heap.

Sift, sift, sift the sand
In my sieve so fine.
The little sand grains come
    right through;
The big ones stay behind.

Barbara Backer

10 Gritty sand can ruin carpets and floors. To cut down on sand carried inside, hang a whisk broom by the outside door. Children develop motor skills when they remove their shoes, empty them, then brush sand from shoes, socks, and clothes before going inside.

Balancing and Swinging

1 Young children are still developing a sense of balance. Introduce your children to creative movement activities that improve their ability to balance.

Flamingo—Each child stands on one leg, arms outstretched, and slowly bends forward from the waist.

Elevator—Each child bends his or her knees and slowly squats down, then comes back up. Children enjoy calling out the floors as they move down and up.

2 Let your children practice balancing on toes, hands, knees, and feet with these activities:

Frog—Each child sits on his or her heels and balances on tiptoe. With arms raised, the child lays both forearms on top of his or her head. Can the child hop on tiptoe?

Cat—Each child begins on hands and knees, then straightens legs and arms while slowly dropping his or her head. The child then returns to the starting position.

3 Have the children balance on one, two, three, or more points. Ask your children to get down on their hands and knees. Then ask them to balance with a particular number of body parts touching the ground. Say, "Can you balance with only three parts on the ground? Three different parts? Two? One? Five?" Discuss the various solutions and accept all efforts.

4 Challenge your children to move while balancing a beanbag on a body part. Let them suggest the part—elbow, head, neck, shoulder, outstretched arm, one foot. Can they move from a standing to a sitting position without dropping their beanbag? From standing up to lying down? Can they hop? Walk backward? Sideways?

5 Give each of your children a large spoon and a tennis ball, golf ball, or Ping-Pong ball. Can they balance the ball in the spoon while walking? Walking backward? Try different balls and different sizes of spoons.

6 Have your children begin and end a movement on signal, moving while you tap out a beat on a small drum or a tambourine. When the sound stops, they should stop. When the sound begins, they should move. Practice first while they move a hand or a foot, then an arm or a leg. Now continue while the children walk, skip, hop, or run forward or backward. Can they feel their muscles work as they try to keep their balance?

7 Practice color recognition and listening skills while balancing. Cut 12-by-2-inch strips from colorful fabric remnants. Tie a different-colored strip to each arm and leg of a child. If desired, tie a longer strip as a headband. While your children move to music, call out a color. Ask the children to move only the body part with that color attached. Sometimes, call out two or more colors.

8 Pumping a swing uses many muscles and requires shifting weight and position at just the right time. Sit on a swing that isn't moving and demonstrate how your motion makes the swing move. Help your children practice with the swing at rest.

9 Singing the following song reminds children of the action needed for pumping the swing.

Sung to: "The Paw Paw Patch"

Lie down with my feet out,
Sit up and put them under me.
Lie down with my feet out,
Sit up and put them under me.

Barbara Backer

10 The area under swings quickly becomes worn from children's digging feet. Children build muscles, coordination, and a sense of responsibility when they help you fill in the holes with loose sand. Be certain there is plenty of loose sand or other spongy material under the swings at all times to cushion falls.

Throwing, Catching, Kicking, and Batting Skills

1 All children need safe and nonthreatening equipment while they are developing motor skills. For beginners who are learning to throw and catch, offer soft, slow-moving sponge balls or beach balls.

2 Give your children time to explore balls freely—one ball per child. Next, have them practice throwing and catching with a partner. Show the children how to use both hands to bat the ball up and then hit it forward like a volleyball.

3 Help your children make lightweight balls of several sizes by stuffing paper bags with crumbled newspaper. Tape the bags shut. Use these to toss, kick, and catch. Throw them at targets or into cardboard cartons.

4 A soft ball made from a sock won't intimidate reluctant ball players. Fill the toe and foot of a heavy sock with discarded pantyhose or discarded socks. Tightly tie the leg of the sock as close to the stuffing as possible. Cut off the sock leg close to the knot. These sock balls are good for beginners. Let children gain skill by throwing toward a large target such as a wall or a fence. Space the children so they are unlikely to be hit while retrieving their balls.

8 Learning to kick a ball takes practice. As a first step, have your children remove their shoes and push a beanbag or sock ball along the floor with their feet. Mark a path on the floor with tape, and let them try to follow the path.

9 When your children are learning to kick, start with large, lightweight balls or other light objects like plastic bottles. Let the children kick in any safe direction.

10 Roll several sheets of newspaper into a tight ball, leaving a corner of one sheet hanging out about 6 inches as a "handle." Secure the ball with masking tape. Tie a cord to the handle, and suspend the ball from the ceiling so it hangs at your children's waist level. Flatten, then roll a large paper grocery bag to form a thin bat. Tape securely. Have the children use the bat to hit the suspended ball. Can they hit it while it is moving?

5 When introducing balls, have at least one for every child and extras for when one goes over the fence. When children have to share balls, those with the least ball-handling skill have little chance to use them. If you have a limited number of balls, send only a few children out to play with them (supervised) at a time.

6 A mitt made from the soft side of Velcro makes it easy for children to catch foam balls or beanbags. These mitts are available from parent-teacher stores or educational surplus catalogs.

7 Use plastic lids from whipped topping containers as Frisbees. After your children have practiced throwing and chasing them for several days, place a Hula Hoop or a beach towel on the ground as a target. How close to the target can the children throw their Frisbees?

Spicing Up
Learning Centers

Art Center

1 Having a place for everything keeps the many materials in your art center organized. Shallow boxes make good containers for clean paper, and a deep container works well for paper scraps. Crayons can be sorted by color and stored in clear plastic cups for easy identification.

2 Try storing art materials in stacking plastic containers with lids. Hot-glue a material (cotton ball, craft stick, pompon, etc.) to each of the outside ends of its container as a label. Use pictures or words to label every container in the art center, and label shelves to show where the containers go.

3 Plastic yogurt containers are great for holding paint at the easel. Cover containers with aluminum foil or their own snap-on lids between uses. Squeeze-top condiment bottles are good for storing paint. Children can squeeze out what they need into the yogurt containers and can learn from mixing colors, too.

4 Children love mixing their own paint! Be sure to mix dry tempera powder with just a bit of water before giving it to your children. (The dry powder can harm children if they inhale it.) Store this "paint paste" in a container with a wide mouth. Let your children measure this mixture with small plastic scoops. Make a picture recipe chart showing the number of scoops of paint and water necessary to make 1/4 cup of paint. Keep this chart and a measuring cup near the sink, and children can mix paint as needed.

5 Children use lots of glue when making collages, leaving large white globs as part of the creation. Plan for this excess glue to become part of the finished artwork. Add a bit of tempera paint to the glue and mix well before using. You can tint the glue to match your children's artwork. Use pink glue for a Valentine's Day card, or blue for an undersea collage.

6 Applying glue from a spout bottle is a skill that develops over time and becomes more refined as coordination develops. To help your children dispense just the right amount of glue, offer them glue in 1.25-ounce bottles. The small bottles are easier for little hands to handle.

7 Collages are a favorite with young children, who enjoy handling materials of various textures and sticking them in glue. Provide paper plates, box lids, or cardboard as a base for a collage. Offer a variety of collage materials, such as corrugated paper; greeting cards; cotton balls; buttons, dyed rice, sand, or pasta; and eggshells.

8 Children like to make drawings of themselves and their families and friends. Provide crayons, markers, and paints in colors that represent a variety of skin tones.

9 The secret to keeping modeling dough fresh is to have children wash their hands thoroughly before playing with it. Add unsweetened powdered drink mix to your favorite modeling dough recipe for bright color and a long-lasting, sweet smell. To add sparkle, sprinkle glitter on the children's workspace before they begin using the modeling dough.

10 Art is an important part of multicultural learning. Throughout the year, display pictures of artwork from other cultures. Look for pictures of paintings, pottery, jewelry, sculptures, and more. Discuss the displays. Help your children see that different artistic styles exist and that all are valued.

Science Center

1 When selecting materials for your science center, build on your children's interests. For instance, if the children enjoy playing with trucks and cars, you might include an assortment of wheels and other rolling objects.

2 Include a variety of materials from your yard in the science center. Different materials will be available at different times of the year. Children love to collect natural treasures, so they will enjoy adding to your collection. Doing so helps them pay closer attention to the world around them. Encourage your children to sort and classify the materials.

3 Provide magnifying glasses and a tray of things to investigate. Change the items whenever you begin a new unit of study. Insects, fabric scraps, leaves, craft sticks, and pictures from the newspaper are just a few suggestions. Display pictures of magnified items. These are often available in children's magazines or puzzle and game magazines. Can your children guess what they are? If possible, display the real item beside the magnified picture.

4 Children are fascinated by their own fingerprints. Have your children examine their fingers under a magnifying glass, then let them use a stamp pad to make fingerprint patterns on paper. Show the children the prints their fingers leave on clean glass objects.

5 Real animals and plants provide many opportunities for exploration and discovery. An aquarium, a classroom pet, or an assortment of potted plants can be a permanent feature of your science center. Encourage your children to observe changes in these living things throughout the year.

6 Collect thick, stretchy socks. Put a familiar item, such as a block, a crayon, or a spoon, into each sock, and tie the opening in a knot. Place these socks in your science center. Let your children feel each one and try to identify the object inside. Make a picture card of each object so the children can match the hidden items with their pictures.

7 Ask your children to bring in a variety of paper: glossy advertisements, gift-wrap, toilet tissue, newspaper, and more. Cut the samples into 2-inch squares, and encourage the children to examine them to determine their differences and similarities. How do they look, feel, and smell? Do they absorb water?

8 Place budding flowers or branches in the science center, where children can watch them change as buds open. Provide paper and crayons for recording observations.

9 Ask parents to donate broken mechanical toys and small appliances for the children to dismantle. Provide real tools in small sizes for your children's use. Cut off power cords from electric appliances before putting them in the science center. Clocks, radios, toasters, mixers, and other kitchen items are a welcome challenge. Ask at a junkyard for an old carburetor. Children will spend days taking it apart.

10 Remember to include books in your science center. A children's librarian can direct you to illustrated nonfiction books about each topic your children study. Even if the text is advanced, children enjoy the colorful pictures.

★ Block Center

1 Your children can make blocks by stuffing empty boxes with wadded newspaper, then taping the boxes shut. Boxes from laundry detergent, diapers, shoes, cereal, pasta, and oatmeal are good choices. Juice boxes make small, standard-size, sturdy blocks.

2 Discarded bed sheets make wonderful working surfaces in the block center. Let your children color the sheets with felt tip markers to make rivers, lakes, forests, and other backgrounds. Old scarves can be used as well.

3 Put carpet squares, sample squares of vinyl flooring, bubble wrap, an indoor-outdoor mat, a sisal door mat, and similar items in the block center to be used as floors, grass, parking lots, or other surfaces. Oatmeal boxes and large coffee cans with both ends removed make excellent tunnels.

4 Provide blocks that reinforce mathematical concepts. By playing with unit blocks, your children will discover that two square blocks of one size are equal to one rectangular one. Triangular and rounded blocks enhance children's understanding of these shapes.

5 Personalize your block area by making a set of "friend blocks" for your children. Tape each child's photo to a homemade or wooden block. Your children will enjoy building with these friendly faces.

6 Children who seldom play in the block center can be enticed by props. Try borrowing dolls, puppets, or costumes from other learning centers. New patterns of play emerge as your children construct a hospital for sick dolls, or build a puppet theater.

7 Film canisters, thread spools, cardboard tubes, cotton batting, and bottle caps are just a few of the things children can use to accessorize block constructions. Show your children how to wrap aluminum foil around blocks and cardboard tubes to make silvery rocket ships, skyscrapers, and other shiny things.

8 Glue a spring-type clothespin, clip end up, to the side of a block to make a sign holder. Provide index cards and pens for your children to use to make signs for their constructions, or let them dictate their words to you: "Fire Station," "Lion's Den," "A unicorn lives here." Use two sign holders side by side for larger signs.

9 Show your children how to build a simple maze by setting up parallel rows of unit blocks. Include one or two simple turns. Have them roll small cars through the maze or blow a Ping-Pong ball through it with a straw. Encourage the children to build mazes for each other. Watch them construct more complicated mazes as their skills grow.

10 Cleaning up the block area can be overwhelming, especially when children have used every block and accessory. Simplify cleanup by storing your blocks on open shelves with a section for each size and shape. On each shelf, tape a tracing of the kind of blocks that belong there. Your children can then match blocks to the outlines on the shelf.

Lion's Den

Sand Table

1 Provide plastic containers that have openings of different sizes: bottles, jars, cups, vials, and so on. Include an empty spice container with a rotating top that offers different pouring options. Encourage your children to discuss which containers take longer to fill and empty.

2 Provide containers of water for moistening the sand. Ask your children to describe how wet sand is different from dry sand. Offer an assortment of sand molds and items to press into moist sand. Margarine tubs, film canisters, gelatin molds, shells, and burlap are good choices. Change these accessories often to challenge the children.

3 Put a dishpan containing about 2 inches of water in the middle of the sand. How does that change the play? It may be different every day. One time the pan might be a pond for dinosaurs and another time your children might add sand to the water until it becomes muck.

4 Empty sand from the sand table and fill it with other materials—birdseed, rice, dried beans or corn, pompons, scarves from garage sales, or plastic-foam chips. If you don't have enough of an item to fill the table, pour the item into one or more dishpans and set these in an empty sand table.

5 Fill your sand table with dirt. Provide a variety of trowels, spades, gardening gloves, a small watering can, and other gardening items. On another day, add planting containers and seeds for each of your children. Fill containers with dirt from the table, then plant the seeds.

9 Hide items in the sand from time to time to spark new enthusiasm for sand play. Buttons, coins, feathers, and seeds work well. Many of these can be sprayed with gold or silver paint to look like valuable treasure—but don't spray everything. Treasure should be a rare find.

10 To keep the area around your sand table clean, provide soft brushes so your children can clean sandy items before putting them away. Also, hang a broom and a dustpan nearby so children can clean the floor around the sand table.

6 Add items to the sand table to enhance your unit of study. Add toy dinosaurs, plastic trees, and real branches to encourage dinosaur play. Molded farm animals, a barn, and a toy tractor support farm play. Ask your children what they think you should add to the sand table during each unit. Let them bring in and play with items from home.

7 Display pictures of roads, cities, and airports near the sand table. Provide small vehicles and road signs to inspire young engineers and architects. Remember to keep paper and pencil nearby so your children can "write" signs for their creations.

8 Challenge your children to make sifters for the sand table. Offer paper, cardboard, aluminum pie plates, margarine tubs and lids, hole punches, hammers and nails (supervise their use), and other materials that the children request. Have the children evaluate their creations. Discuss which sifters work best.

Water Table

1 Provide a variety of items for water play, but don't set out everything on the same day. Plastic measuring cups, jars, and bottles encourage pouring and measuring. Include some funnels and clear plastic tubing, and use duct tape to attach a tube to one or two funnels. Ketchup bottles and liquid dishwashing detergent bottles provide squirting fun, while pie pans, milk cartons, and sieves support other learning.

2 Plain water is inviting to children, but if interest lags, add enticing things to attract your children to the water table. Suggestions include glitter and sequins, snips of yarn and thread, large buttons, plastic snap-together cubes, a variety of classroom items that sink and float, and potpourri or perfume (be certain no one is allergic to fragrances).

3 While your children are playing, add a few drops of food coloring to the water. Children enjoy mixing it in. On another day, add several colors, each at different places in the water. Children are enchanted by the changes as they mix the colors. Add liquid dishwashing detergent and offer egg beaters, whisks, or straws for making bubbles.

4 Freeze water in gelatin molds or in other plastic containers of all shapes and sizes. Unmold the ice shapes and float them in the water for a cooling treat on a hot day. If you wish, add food coloring to the water before freezing it in the molds. Use two primary colors, and watch as your children discover what happens when melting ice of different colors combines.

5 Children enjoy washing things. Set several dishpans of soapy water and a dish drainer inside an empty water table. Provide sponges, dish mops, brushes, and towels, and encourage your children to wash and dry classroom toys, blocks, or dishes from the dramatic play center.

6 Colds and other viruses spread rapidly in school settings. Prevent the spread of germs by having your children wash their hands thoroughly before participating in water play. Some teachers add a small amount of chlorinated bleach to the water table. Follow directions on the bottle, remembering that children put wet hands in their mouths. Be certain the amounts you use are safe.

7 Slimy textures are fun for children. Set several dishpans in an empty water table. In each pan, mix one part corn starch and two parts water. The result is a substance that seems both liquid and solid.

8 Provide full-length plastic aprons to help keep your children's clothes dry. Show the children how to roll up or push up their sleeves, or use sweat bands or garters to hold up their sleeves. Promote cooperation by encouraging the children to help one another with sleeves and with putting on aprons.

9 Children learn responsibility when they help clean up. Hang child-size mops, thick towels, and sponges near the water table so children can dry each item before putting it away. Have sufficient space for storing all equipment.

10 If you don't have a water table, set out dishpans of water on tables or on upside-down milk crates. These are easily set up outside, too.

Math Center

1 Have your children and their parents save and bring in items for sorting, counting, and patterning. Ask for items such as bottle tops, jar lids, old keys, pompons, dried beans, shells, rocks, or bread tags. Store each type of item in a separate container, and label containers for easy cleanup. Hot-glue an item to the outside of its container for a label. Children can practice sorting skills as they put items away!

2 Decorative calendar numbers (available from parent-teacher stores) make great number cards for activities and games. Children can put them in sequence or place a corresponding number of items on each numeral. Change the cards regularly to match your seasonal themes. If you attach sandpaper or the hook side of Velcro to the backs of these number cards, they'll stick to a flannelboard.

3 Gather four identical cottage cheese containers and lids. Place ½ cup rice in one container, 1½ cups rice in another, 1 cup salt or sand in another, and leave one empty. Glue the lids on. Have your children pick up the containers and feel their weight, then arrange them in order from lightest to heaviest.

4 Collect a variety of objects for your children to weigh on a balance. Some suggested items are a plastic lemon, a lemon-size rock, a large shell, a small can of food, and a block. Display these with a balance. Make measuring cards as shown in the illustration. Show your children how to compare two items by placing them on the balance and then setting each on the corresponding half of the card. Encourage the children to predict results and test their predictions.

5 Take a survey each day in the math center. Ask your children a yes or no question such as "Do you have a pet? Did you eat breakfast today? Is there a baby at your house? Do your shoes have laces? Do you like to eat spinach?" During circle time, discuss the question.

Make up a survey sheet as shown in the illustration. During center time, have each child make a mark under YES or NO on the survey sheet to record his or her answer. At the end of center time, call a group meeting to tally and discuss the results of the survey. How many children have a pet? How many do not? Which group is larger? Which is smaller?

Do You Have A Pet?	
YES	NO
☺	Laura
	Kwilon
x	
☺	
PAUL	

6 Incorporate fine-motor activities into math center learning. Include Geoboards (boards that have nails hammered in a square grid pattern, one inch apart) and rubber bands of several colors and thicknesses. Let the children use the rubber bands to make shapes. Compare the shapes. Are all squares the same size? All triangles have three sides, but do they all look the same?

7 Because young children are egocentric, they especially enjoy activities centered around them. In winter, have your children bring their gloves or mittens into the room. (Label each with masking tape.) Mix up the mittens and let the children use them as a matching game.

8 Measure each of your children with a long strip of paper. Cut the paper to the child's height and cover it with clear self-stick paper. Put the strips in the math center for the children to explore. They will compare strips to see who is taller or shorter.

9 Mount the strips from the previous tip side by side on a wall of the math center, with the bottom of the strips at floor level. Children can walk up to the display and compare their height with their own and other children's strips.

10 When you put several sets of dominoes in the math center, your children will invent activities using them. Some children will match identical dominoes; those who are ready will count dots; others will match the dominoes end to end.

Music and Movement Center

1 Musical instruments needn't be expensive. Shop at garage sales and thrift stores for tambourines, small drums, real guitars, rain sticks, and other music makers. Common household items also make good instruments. A pot lid hit with a kitchen spoon makes an impressive sound; two wooden spoons hit together make a soothing one.

2 Children enjoy making rhythm instruments for the music and movement center. Have your children string several large jingle bells onto long pipe cleaners. Twist the ends of the pipe cleaners into a handle. Or have the children decorate empty milk jugs and drop bells inside. They can hold these instruments by the handles and shake them to make rhythmic sounds.

3 Have each of your children put a handful of dried beans, pebbles, paper clips, or nails in a long-necked plastic bottle. Glue on the lid. The long neck becomes a handle when you turn the bottle upside down. Make similar shaking instruments with small, plastic soft-drink bottles. Children can see through these to watch the contents shake.

4 Are you running out of shelf space for instruments? Hang your instruments from yarn loops on a pegboard. Outline each instrument to indicate where it belongs, as shown in the illustration. Arrange the instruments on the pegboard by category and size to foster your children's sorting and seriation skills.

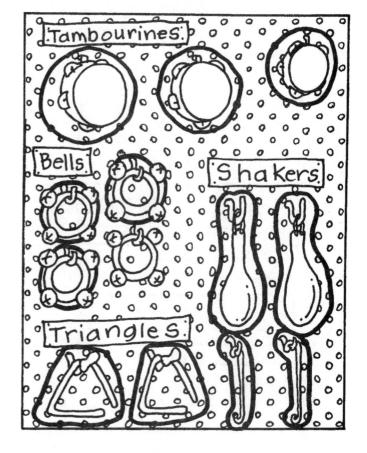

5 Provide a tape player and cassettes with music of many cultures for your children to hear. Offer drums, bells, rhythm sticks, rain sticks, and other rhythm instruments for accompaniment.

9 In the music and movement center, display pictures that relate to your unit of study. Challenge your children to move like the person or thing in the picture—community helpers, jungle animals, dinosaurs, or airplanes. Laminate the pictures, and store previous ones in the center to spark impromptu movement activities.

10 Children appreciate music that is sung just for them. Tape-record yourself or another teacher singing a few of your children's favorite songs. Make the tape a permanent part of your music and movement center. You might become your children's favorite recording star!

6 Include an assortment of scarves in your music and movement center. Garage sales and thrift stores are good sources for these. Your children can use the scarves as impromptu costumes, or as props for dancing.

7 Dancing with streamers extends a child's movements and encourages graceful motions. Strips of fabric remnants make colorful streamers, and lengths of tinsel garlands make sparkly ones.

8 Place a full-length mirror in your music and movement center so your children can watch themselves as they move. You may want to share this mirror with the dramatic play center. Take photographs of the children while they are "dancing" or moving to music. Display these in the music and movement center.

Language Center

1 Set up a reading area as part of the language center. Provide one or two child-size chairs, or put a few cushions on the floor for lounging. Place group-made books and library books on a bookshelf or in a milk crate beside the chairs. Include a favorite stuffed animal that children can read to. Decorate the language center to complement your learning theme: If you are studying beaches, include a beach umbrella, two beach chairs, and a beach bag containing sunglasses, empty sunscreen bottles, and a few magazines.

2 Turn milk crates on their sides to make an impromptu puppet stage. Include a variety of puppets—those that are commercially available and those you and your children make for the language center. Add laminated posters that show step-by-step directions for making simple puppets from paper bags, paper plates, or craft sticks. Children can take a poster to the art center to make the suggested puppet, then return to the language center to let the puppet perform. Provide paper and pens so they can make tickets and small posters for puppet shows.

3 Recycle tattered and worn picture books by cutting out the pictures of the story's characters and turning them into flannelboard figures. Glue the pictures onto heavy paper, cover them with clear self-stick paper, then attach a piece of sandpaper to the back. Store related pictures in zippered plastic bags. Children will use the characters to retell familiar stories or to make up new ones. Don't despair if your children mix up the figures. Putting Red Riding Hood in the brick house with the Three Little Pigs leads to creative thinking.

4 Children develop math vocabulary when you use the flannelboard for math activities. Cut out felt numerals. Glue a small piece of Velcro (hook side) to each of a variety of pompons. Have the children place the numerals on the board, and then stick a matching number of pompons on each numeral.

5 Cut a variety of felt geometric shapes for the flannelboard. At first, your children will place them on the board at random. After a day or two of this, show them how to combine shapes to make other things—two triangles (wings) and a circle (body) for a bat, a triangle and a rectangle for an evergreen tree, etc. Ask them for suggestions.

6 Place a tape player with headphones in the language center as a listening area. Purchase storybook and tape packages or make your own by recording yourself as you read a favorite book. When it's time to turn the page say, "Turn the page," then wait a few seconds before proceeding with the story. Package the tape and book together in a zippered plastic bag. Put a small sticker on each tape and a matching sticker on the book cover to help children with cleanup.

7 Record your own voice as you read a chart story or a rhyme you've written on a chart. Repeat the reading several times. Put the tape and the chart in the listening area so children who want to take a turn can "read along" as they listen to the tape. The many repetitions lead to more proficient pre-reading skills.

8 Turn on the tape recorder during circle time or center time. Put the recorded tape in the listening area and tell your children there is a surprise on the tape. They enjoy hearing their own voices, identifying each other's voices, and hearing favorite circle time activities again.

9 Use the side of a filing cabinet as a magnetboard. Put magnetic letters and numerals there. Collect a variety of matching refrigerator magnets, including some with written advertising. Children can match magnets or put the right number of magnets by each numeral. They also can use magnetic letters to spell out words they see on the advertising magnets.

10 Set up a desk or small table as a writing area, and stock it with paper, pencils, pens, markers, and message pads. Include wooden letters to trace and sandpaper letters to feel. Add a write-on calendar and used appointment books. If possible, set out a typewriter from a garage sale or thrift store and lots of typing paper.

Dramatic Play Center

4 Hang a battery-operated clock at your children's eye level in the kitchen area of the dramatic play center. Provide a wall calendar and an appointment book, complete with pen for writing important dates. Keep a real memo pad, pen, and phone book beside the telephone.

5 Children enjoy using real appliances that are usually hands-off to them. Collect discarded appliances, and cut off the electric cords right where they come out of the appliance. Include toasters, electric frying pans, steamers, hand mixers, alarm clocks, and electric razors. A discarded real microwave oven is more fun (and less expensive) than a wooden pretend one.

1 Provide plastic foods and real pots and pans to cook them in. Add standard-size kitchen spoons and utensils for stirring and cooking. Include foods and cooking utensils that represent different cultures, such as a taco press, a wok, and a frying pan.

2 Shop at garage sales for inexpensive, authentic props. Look for tap and ballet shoes, scarves, hats, necklaces, rings, bracelets, clip earrings, pots and cooking utensils, small appliances, baskets, cameras, wallets, briefcases, calculators, telephones, typewriters, multiethnic clothing and cooking items, dishtowels, and more.

3 Provide multiethnic dolls, including an infant-size baby doll. Buy real baby clothes, baby blankets, a highchair, toys, stroller, and a diaper bag at garage sales, or ask parents for donations. Add newborn-size diapers. Set up a dishpan of soapy water for children to wash baby dolls and their clothes. Provide towels for drying babies and a drying rack for the clothes.

6 Many costume rental stores and formal wear shops hold annual sales where you can purchase stained and damaged costumes at reasonable prices. Check in the Yellow Pages for the location of the shop nearest you. Look for costumes in the smallest possible sizes. You can alter these costumes easily with pinking shears. Simply cut sleeves, pant legs, and skirts to size.

7 Change the dramatic play center to reflect the topics you and your children are exploring. Are you studying food? Turn your center into a grocery store complete with (empty) food cans (use pliers to crimp sharp edges); food boxes; plastic bottles that contained syrup, soda, or liquid dishwashing detergent; grocery bags; cash register and/or hand-held calculators; and baskets to carry the food in.

8 Remember to include clothing that is representative of cultures around the world as well as clothing worn in your own neighborhood. Remember that urban life represents a different culture to suburban children, and vice versa. Be certain your dramatic play center reflects the experience of all the children in your group.

9 Survey parents to learn what holidays your children observe. Invite parents with interesting cultural traditions to visit your program to tell about a special holiday and show some of its ceremonial items. Put holiday items in the dramatic play center when you discuss the celebrations, then leave them for the children to use throughout the year. Borrowed items, of course, must be returned promptly, but perhaps children can make models of them from clay, wood, or other materials.

10 Clean the items in your dramatic play center regularly. Use a disinfectant cleaner on plastic and metal items. Wash everything with hot water. Even if clothing shrinks or fades, it will still be fine for dress up.

Creating Theme Environments

Dinosaur Days

Dinosaurs fascinate children. The huge beasts spark imagination and breathe excitement into learning. Create an environment where dinosaurs are free to roam in children's imaginations and where dinosaur activities bring history to life.

1 Hang a huge dinosaur banner outside your door with a sign reading, "The Land of Dinosaurs." Banners are commercially available, or your children can make one by painting a huge dinosaur that you've sketched on a bed sheet. To give the feeling of a prehistoric environment, hang paper vines from the top of the door frame so the children will pass through the vines as they enter the room.

2 Discuss plants that lived when the dinosaurs lived. Bring several varieties of ferns to show your children. Let them examine the plants with a magnifying glass. Encourage them to compare and contrast the different plants.

If vines grow nearby, bring some in, or take the children to see them. You can also make vines by cutting ³/₄-inch-wide strips of brown or black paper. Have your children attach green paper leaves to both sides of each strip. Hang different lengths of vines from your room's ceiling.

3 Have your children make a dinosaur mural. Help them brainstorm about what they want to include and how they could make those things. Together, look at picture-book illustrations for ideas. For instance, your children could fingerpaint a background and use dinosaur-shaped sponges to make prints on the foreground. Tissue paper leaves and real twigs add to the fun.

4 Let your children be paleontologists for a day. Hide chicken bones around your room for your children to discover. (Disinfect the bones beforehand by boiling them for 20 minutes, then soaking them overnight in a 10 percent bleach solution.) Have the children glue their finds to a paper dinosaur shape.

5 Set up a dinosaur museum. Invite your children to bring toy dinosaurs from home to put on display, or to exhibit dinosaurs they've sculpted from clay. Label all items with the dinosaur's name and the contributor's name. Let the children help make the labels. Accept all attempts, from scribbles and invented spelling to copied words.

6 Children enjoy moving like dinosaurs to music. Any plodding music works well. "Bydlo" from Moussorgsky's *Pictures at an Exhibition* and "Fossils" from Saint-Saëns' *Carnival of the Animals* are good choices.

7 Songs such as the following one engage children's imaginations.

Sung to: "If I Had a Hammer"

If I had a dinosaur,
I'd ride it in the morning.
I'd ride it in the evening,
All over this land.
We'd climb up mountains,
And slide down into valleys,
And sing this happy song all day long,
All over this land.

Barbara Backer

8 Extend this theme to the sand table by putting plastic dinosaurs in the sand. Your children will find ways to add swamps and other features. Have them create more dinosaurs, plants, volcanoes, and other items from paper, boxes, glue, and other art materials. All can become part of the sand table environment.

9 Together, make a huge stuffed dinosaur. Cut two identical dinosaur paper shapes, taller than your children, out of butcher paper. Lay one on top of the other and mark the "inside" and "outside" of each. Have your children paint the outside. Next, have them spread glue around the edges of one unpainted side, leaving openings at the top and bottom. Lay the second dinosaur on top of the first, and seal the glued edges. Have the children fill the dinosaur shape with crumpled newspaper and glue it shut. Lean your creation against a wall or hang it from the ceiling so its feet just touch the floor.

10 Children better understand fossil remains when they create their own. Show them how to make fossil imprints by pressing plastic dinosaurs into modeling dough.

Farm

If at all possible, take a trip to a working farm to see how vegetables grow and to observe farm animals close-up. Watch the farmer milk a cow or a goat, and let your children have a turn, too. When you return to your room, dig into these farm-related activities.

1 Decorate your door to look like a barn door. If you have room, cut a large barn shape from butcher paper and attach it around the door. Add a sign: "Welcome to Our Farm."

2 Decorate your room with several bales of hay. You can get these at a feed store. Put work gloves, overalls, boots, straw hats, and plastic fruits and vegetables in the dramatic play center. To extend the mood, try wearing overalls and a straw hat!

3 Place a toy barn, plastic animals, and toy pickup trucks and tractors in the block center. Add empty oatmeal containers for silos and blue or brown fabric for a pond. Wooden cubes or spools and plastic-foam chips can be loaded on trucks and wagons. Shredded paper can be hay for the animals.

4 Have your children work together to make a scarecrow. Brainstorm to decide what you will need and how you will go about making one. It's fun to make several scarecrows so everyone has a greater opportunity to be involved, so how about creating a scarecrow family? Discuss the scarecrow's job on the farm. What other ways might farmers protect their crops?

5 Sing "Old MacDonald Had a Farm" together. After the usual verses, ask your children what else Farmer MacDonald might have had on his farm. A TV? A teddy bear? Red pajamas? Encourage creative thinking. Now sing the song again. Ask each child in turn to suggest a new verse.

Later, have your children make a group book about Old MacDonald's Farm. Let each child make one page of the book by drawing a picture of something Old MacDonald had on his farm. (Accept all answers. Unusual responses add humor to the song.) Add words, and gather the pages into a book. The children will enjoy following the book as they sing the song.

6 Make a farm scene on the wall. Discuss what is found on the farm. Then set out precut shapes of these items for your children to decorate. (Older children can draw and cut out their own.) Have your children glue their creations to the mural. Increase interest by adding other textures to the scene. Craft sticks make good fences, and holograph gift-wrap works well as a pond with sunshine reflecting from it. Label the board "Old MacDonald's Farm," or any name the children choose. Label parts of the scene as you wish.

7 Use die-cut paper animal shapes to make math games. Write one numeral (0 to 9) on each of ten shapes. Cover the shapes with clear self-stick paper. Ask your children to place the shapes in numerical order, or to "feed the animals" by putting the corresponding number of kernels of dried corn on each animal.

These animal shapes can be used with songs, as well. Using a variety of animal shapes, distribute one shape to each child. As you sing "Old MacDonald Had a Farm," have the children hold up the animal mentioned in each verse and make that animal's sound.

8 To show the variety of things that come from farms, make a display of farm-produced items. Cover a table with a farm print or vegetable print fabric. Put out fresh and canned fruits and vegetables, empty milk cartons, egg cartons, cottage cheese containers, bread wrappers, wool clothing, and other items. Discuss the items and how they relate to farms. Sort and classify the items together.

9 Look for pictures of farm animals in discarded books and magazines and in parent-teacher stores. Illustrated brochures on farming are available from your county cooperative extension office. Mount these pictures on heavy paper and use them for an assortment of activities.

10 Fill your room with the aroma of fruits and vegetables while your children prepare each day's snack. Ask each child to bring in a piece of fresh fruit. Have the children wash and cut the fruit to make fruit salad. Use plastic knives with serrated blades for safe cutting. On another day, have children wash and tear lettuce for a green salad.

Outer Space

Outer space is dark and quiet. When people travel there, they float, moving slowly in their weightless state. It sounds like a teacher's dream environment! Transform your room into a space scene, and remind your children to float quietly when they move around the room.

1 Spread dark butcher paper on the floor, and invite your children to make a space mural. (Cover surrounding areas, and put smocks on the children to protect them from flying paint.) Show your children how to dip a brush in paint and flick their wrist to make a spatter design on the paper. Use several colors of paint to create a vibrant night sky. When this dries, it becomes the background paper for your mural.

2 Display your space background on the wall at your children's eye level. Have the children add self-stick stars and triangle and rectangle shapes cut from holograph gift-wrap or aluminum foil. Let them glue these to the background paper to make rocket ships.

3 Post a space rhyme, such as the following one, near your display. Help your children learn the words and encourage them to act out the rhyme with creative movement.

I want to be an astronaut
And fly up to the moon.
I'll soar around the Milky Way
And won't come back 'til June.

Barbara Backer

4 Stimulate your children to build space constructions by putting pictures of planets, space stations, and satellites in the block center. Show the children how to make silvery building blocks by wrapping aluminum foil around blocks or oatmeal boxes.

Have your children make space stations by gluing empty boxes and cartons together. When the glue dries, they can paint their creations or wrap them with aluminum foil. Children can work alone or in pairs or small groups. Place the completed creations around the room. Hang some from the ceiling as if in orbit.

Fill your room with astronauts. Trace around each child's body on butcher paper. Cut out the resulting figures. Have your children draw in their facial features. Suggest that they also color the feet and hands to look like boots and gloves, and add buttons, gauges, and hoses to the body to make it look like a space suit. Hang the figures from the ceiling with thread. Hang some upside down, and hang some by their feet or by their sides so all appear weightless.

Add "spacewear" to your dramatic play area. Apply reflective tape to oversize T-shirts to make costumes. Helmets can be as simple as aluminum colanders, or they can be made by cutting the bottom and side from a gallon bleach bottle. You can also make a helmet by cutting a hole (face shield) in the side of a cardboard ice cream tub.

Fill your reading area with fiction and nonfiction books about space. Books written for older children have wonderful pictures for little ones.

Make satellites to hang from the ceiling. Have your children paint round wooden toothpicks with white tempera paint. Dry these on waxed paper overnight. The following day, the children can poke the toothpicks into plastic-foam balls.

Decorate a sweatshirt or T-shirt to wear while your children study space. Cut star shapes from gold and silver fabric. Use fusible webbing to appliqué these to a dark shirt. Outline the stars with glittery fabric paint. Clerks in a fabric or craft shop can show you this easy process in a few minutes.

Polar Regions

The Arctic and Antarctic regions seem barren, but many animals and plants live there. The polar regions are fun to study in summer or winter. Add excitement by having your children prepare for a make-believe expedition.

1 Place a "Polar Expeditions" sign on your door. Write each child's name on a small pennant shape and arrange these near the sign. Display pictures of Arctic animals on one side of the room and Antarctic animals on the other.

Have your children talk about an "expedition" and what explorers need to take along. Put sunglasses, warm hats, boots, parkas, and other props in the dramatic play center. Provide discarded cameras (without film) so explorers can photograph their discoveries, and clipboards and pens so they can write reports.

2 Place some small pillows on a table and drape a white sheet over all to simulate snow and icy ground. Drape blue scarves over part of this for water. Have your children fashion polar animals from modeling dough to put in the display. Add vinyl animals and fish. Challenge your children to think of other things to add and ways to make them.

3 Use pictures of polar animals for graphing activities. Help your children categorize the animals according to color, number of legs, or other characteristics.

4 Cut easel paper in the shapes of polar animals. The cut paper can be used for other activities. Record stories of whales on whale-shaped paper and descriptions of penguins on penguin-shaped paper.

5 Polar animals move in strange and wonderful ways. For instance, the penguin is a flightless bird. Seals, so sleek and graceful in the water, lumber awkwardly on land with only their flippers to propel them. Polar bears are powerful swimmers with giant paws for sure footing on the ice. Have your children imitate these and other polar creatures as you play "The Skater's Waltz" or other instrumental music.

8 It's easy to show children how camouflage protects animals. Give your children precut polar animal shapes. (Older children may want to cut out their own.) Animals that are always white or that turn white for the winter should be cut from white paper. Other animals should be cut from colored paper or colored by the children. Have the children glue their shapes to white paper. Then have them view the creation from a distance. What do they see?

9 Put molded vinyl polar animals in your block center or water table. Sets (available from parent-teacher stores) include polar bears, penguins, whales, and more. In the water table, challenge children to construct ice and land for the land animals. Offer milk jugs, plastic bottles and other containers for their use. Help the children brainstorm how they can create a polar environment in the block center. Offer scarves, fabric, and cotton batting.

6 Simulate icebergs in the water table. Freeze water in a variety of plastic containers, large and small. Float the resulting ice shapes in the water table. Provide terry towels and basins of warm water to heat your children's hands after they play in the icy water.

7 Add a freezing touch to a matching game. Freeze water in a variety of small, medium, and large plastic containers. Include small and extra-large margarine tubs and 1-, 2-, and 3-quart plastic bowls. Unmold the ice onto cafeteria trays and have your children match each ice block to its mold. They'll play with these for hours, and will enjoy predicting which ice blocks will melt first and last.

10 Fill your reading area with books about the geography, plants, and animals of polar regions.

Desert

There are deserts around the world. It's best to pick one area to discuss, and these suggestions are based on animals and plants in the Sonoran Desert of the southwestern United States. Use these tips to help you re-create the desert in your room.

1 Have your children make a desert scene as a large mural or a bulletin board. This is a week-long project. Begin by having the children paint the background. For a mottled, sunbleached, or moon-kissed look, dip small oval sponges into tempera paint. Press these to the background paper in a random pattern using sky tones on the upper half of the paper and earth tones below. Put sand in the earth-tone paints to add texture to the mural. Since most desert animals stay hidden during the hot daylight hours, consider making a nighttime scene that includes nocturnal animals and night-blooming plants.

2 As your children learn about desert plants and animals, have them glue cutouts of these flora and fauna to the mural. If desired, the children can color them first. Glue some of the figures to small pieces of cardboard and then to the mural to make them stick out from the surface. Cut cactus shapes from corrugated cardboard. Have the children paint them green, then add small tissue paper flowers. Together, look in books and at nature videos for other ideas.

3 Children like to play with rubber stamps. Look for rubber stamps of desert plants and animals, including desert flowers, saguaro cacti, coyotes, snakes, and owls. Your children can use the stamps to decorate the mural, and you can use them to make learning games.

4 Children are captivated by the unusual, so they really like learning about the large saguaro cactus. Native to the Americas, it is actually a tree. Give your children large sheets of green paper cut into saguaro cactus shapes. Let them glue broken toothpicks to the paper for prickly cactus spines. Hang the completed pictures around your room to surround your learning area with these gentle giants.

5 Bring several types of cacti, including some that blossom, into the room. Use these real cacti for math activities. Have your children arrange them in order by height, or sort them into two categories: those that are blooming and those that are not.

8 Put desert animal puppets or stuffed animals in the language center. Place plastic animals in the sand table and the block center. Encourage your children to make cacti from green modeling dough to add to the sand table or block center.

9 Cut cactus shapes from green felt. Write a number (0 to 5, or 0 to 10) on each. Cut small flower shapes. Put cactus and flowers at the flannelboard. Have your children put the correct number of flowers on each cactus.

10 Become part of the desert environment. Purchase or decorate a T-shirt or sweatshirt to wear while teaching about the desert. Wildlife organizations have many attractive shirts available. To decorate your own, select a beige shirt. Cut a saguaro cactus shape from green fabric and attach the shape to the shirt with fusible webbing. Outline the cactus shape with green fabric paint. (Get directions and supplies at a fabric or craft store.)

6 Take the opportunity to explore and discuss texture with your children. Have the children examine the prickly surface of a cactus with a magnifying glass. Let them gently touch the plant's sharp spines. Use the word *prickly* to describe the cactus. Then play the following game.

Gather some prickly items, like a brush, a pine cone, and a plastic fork. Place them in a container with a variety of soft items, like a mitten, a stuffed animal, and a cotton ball. Let your children sort the items according to their texture.

7 Use a copy machine with enlarging and reducing capabilities to make several sizes of cactus or animal pictures. Use these as patterns for flannelboard figures. Have your children place the figures on the flannelboard in order from smallest to largest (or largest to smallest). Cut out same-size figures, too, for patterning activities.

Ranch

Ranch life and ranch workers captivate the imagination of young children. But cowpokes are real people whose protective clothing and unique tools enable them to do the hard work necessary to raise livestock. As your children study ranch life, they'll learn to respect these workers and value their work in a new way.

1 Cover your door with butcher paper. Have your children decide on a name for the group's ranch, and write "Welcome to the _____ Ranch" on the butcher paper. Provide precut cowboy, horse, and cattle figures for the children to color and glue to the paper. (Older children can draw and cut out their own figures.)

2 Western-wear catalogs are filled with pictures of people in cowboy garb. Send for a few of these catalogs before you begin your ranch unit. You can use the pictures for flannelboard stories, art projects, learning games, and many other activities.

3 Buy or cut out paper boot and hat shapes to use for matching and patterning games.

4 Ask your children to bring in yardsticks. Provide extras for children who forget. Give the children precut horse head shapes. (Older children can draw and cut out their own.) Have the children decorate the heads with markers or crayons. They can glue on yarn snips for a mane, if desired. With glue or masking tape, attach each head to the end of a yardstick to make a hobby horse. The children can "ride" their horses indoors or out.

5 Cattle brands, with their distinctive symbols, can be the basis for a variety of activities. Display pictures of cattle brands in your writing area for your children to copy. Challenge the children to create their own cattle brands. What do the symbols mean? Make a set of cattle brand cards for use in matching and memory games.

6 Include props such as bandannas, cowboy hats, vests, a sheriff's badge, a frying pan, cooking utensils, a canteen, rope, and hobby horses in your dramatic play center.

7 Cowboys like to sing. Write this song on a chart and point to the words as your children sing. Let the children take turns wearing a cowboy hat and leading the group. The leader makes a motion, and the children copy the motion while everyone sings. The leader gives the hat to another child, who becomes the next leader.

Sung to: "Did You Ever See a Lassie?"

Did you ever see a cowboy,
A cowboy, a cowboy?
Did you ever see a cowboy
Go this way and that?
Go this way and that way?
Go that way and this way?
Did you ever see a cowboy
Go this way and that?

Repeat the song for each child, substituting *cowgirl* for *cowboy* as necessary.

Barbara Backer

8 Snacks are a must on the hot, dusty trail. Set out several different kinds of dried fruit, seeds, and cereal pieces, each in a separate bowl. Select a large plastic bag and let each of your children scoop an ingredient into it. Shake the bag thoroughly to mix. Have each cowpoke remove a scoop of the finished mix and put it into his or her own zippered sandwich bag for nourishment on the trail (or playground).

9 Because clothesline is thick but soft, it's easy to untie knots in it. Cut several lengths of line. Dip half of each length into diluted food coloring; remove, and dry. The different-colored ends help your children see what happens when they tie knots. All of this tying and untying develops fine motor skills.

10 Cut cowboy and cowgirl figures from felt for use on the flannelboard. Include felt hats, jackets, vests, boots, and other clothing items. Let your children take turns dressing the figures, naming each article of clothing as they put it on.

Pond

Whether located in a national forest, in a local park, or at the back of a shopping center, ponds are marvelous habitats that are rich in plant and animal life. There are many small animals to investigate and lots of intriguing flying and swimming insects. Bring the pond environment into your room with these tips.

1 Take your children to see a real pond, if possible. Discuss the animals and plants you see there. Which are in the water and which are on the shore? Then work together to create a pond scene in your room. Draw a large oval for a pond at the bottom corner of a piece of white butcher paper. Have your children add a sky and shore to this scene. They can glue small pieces of blue and green tissue paper to the pond for water. Cattails and other grasses can be painted with cotton swabs, and animals can be sponge-painted at the water's edge. (Look for animal sponges at parent-teacher and craft stores.) Real leaves and twigs add to the environment. Encourage your children to contribute their ideas.

2 Have your children name the parts of the pond mural. Help them make a label for each part.

3 There are many colorful fabrics with prints of pond animals and flowers. These can be used in many ways: to cover bulletin boards, doors, and tables; as blankets and costumes for dramatic play; or as a work surface for the block center. You can cut figures from these fabrics to use as appliqués for a T-shirt, a sweatshirt, or an apron.

4 Bring the pond to the flannelboard. Cut five felt frog shapes of various sizes. Have your children arrange them in order from smallest to largest. Cut out a log and a "pond" shape. Put the frogs on the log and count the frogs as the children sing "Five Little Speckled Frogs" or another counting song.

5 It's fun to move like pond animals. Hopping frogs and toads, darting dragonflies, slithering snakes, and quacking ducks delight young children. Take movement activities outdoors when weather permits.

6 Turn your water table into a simulated pond. Put models of pond animals in the water. Add real leaves and twigs, and float plastic ducks on top.

9 Children love to go fishing in a make-believe pond. To make a fishing pole, string a small magnet from the end of a wooden dowel. Cut fish shapes from various colors of construction paper. Put a paper clip on the nose of each fish. To make a pond, spread a blue towel on the floor and scatter the fish on it. Let your children take turns dipping the pole into the pond. While one child fishes, the remaining children can sing the following song.

Sung to: "The Farmer in the Dell"

I can catch a fish.
I can catch a fish.
Put in my line, and I'll do fine.
I can catch a fish.

Barbara Backer

7 Float water lilies in your water-table pond. To make the flowers, cut two individual cups from a plastic-foam egg carton. Cut each section into a lily shape. Put one inside the other and push a brass paper fastener through the bottom of the blossom to attach it to a base cut from a plastic-foam food tray.

8 Bring an empty plastic wading pool into your room, along with a few plastic fish, frogs, and plants. Your children will spend hours playing in this "pond," and they may even think of new accessories to add.

10 Help your children take a survey to discover which is your group's favorite pond animal. Have them narrow the field to two or three candidates. Make a chart with a column for each animal. Draw or glue a picture of each animal to the top of its column. Have each child make a mark in one column to vote for his or her favorite. Tally the votes and discuss the results.

The Seashore

The edge of the sea draws people with its beauty and its magical qualities. What is seen one hour may not be there the next. The shore is always changing. Help your children learn to love the shore and its beauty, and teach them the value of preserving the beach.

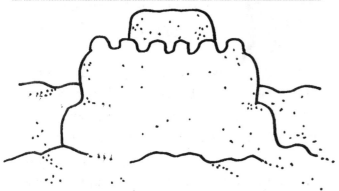

1 Children (and adults) love to build sand castles. Put plastic containers of various shapes and sizes in the outdoor sandbox and the indoor sand table. Dampen the sand so it will hold its shape. Show your children how to pack damp sand into the containers and then unmold it. Display pictures of sand castles to inspire young builders.

2 Beachcombing is part of the fun of a trip to the shore. Bury seashells in your sand area or hide them around the room for your children to discover. Set a few shells in your water table for the children to brush clean.

3 Put out a dishpan full of seashells for your children to explore. Encourage the children to sort the shells, arrange them from largest to smallest or from darkest to lightest, use them for patterning, match them to numerals, and more.

4 The surf rubs holes in some seashells. Put these in the art center for painting and stringing into necklaces and bracelets.

5 Together, create a seashore mural or a bulletin board display. Add sand to the paint for the shore. Provide real seashells for gluing along the sand. Encourage your children to add pictures of sea animals and birds to the display.

6 Craft stores and parent-teacher stores sell sponges cut into shapes of shells and seashore animals. Purchase a few (or cut your own from a plain kitchen sponge). Use them for sponge-painting critters directly onto the mural, or have the children print them onto easel paper, then continue painting at the easel.

9 Set up a terrarium for hermit crabs (available at pet stores) and display them in your room. Your children can take turns feeding them and changing their water. Put empty shells in the terrarium and watch to see which shells the crabs select to live in as they grow.

10 Make a bottle full of ocean waves for your children to play with. Fill a plastic soda bottle two-thirds full with water tinted with blue food coloring. Fill the bottle to the top with mineral oil, leaving no air in the bottle. Screw the bottle securely shut, sealing it with glue, and wrap the cap with duct tape to discourage the children from trying to open it. Check the bottle daily to be certain the duct tape is tightly sealed. To create waves, hold the bottle on its side and gently rock it back and forth.

7 Children are surprised to learn that huge turtles live in the ocean. These animals come onto shore to lay their eggs. Have your children make turtles to place around the room. Turn a paper bowl upside down, and paint it for the turtle's shell. Cut out feet, a head, and a tail from construction paper and glue them in place.

8 Put a few beach chairs and a beach umbrella in your language center to transform it into a sunny beach. Include props such as a beach towel, sunglasses, a beach hat, empty sunscreen bottles, sports drink bottles, sandals, and a few magazines in a beach bag. Display books about the seashore in this center.

Under the Sea

There is more water than land on Earth, and the largest bodies of water are the oceans. They are full of plant and animal life. Transform your room into an underwater wonderland while you learn about life under the sea. Plan to spend several weeks on this project.

1 Cover the ceiling with blue paper, the windows with blue plastic food wrap, and tables with underwater-print fabric. Have your children decorate the room with paper fish and other sea creatures. Show your children how to make translucent jellyfish by squirting blobs of white glue onto waxed paper, then sprinkling a bit of glitter on the glue. Let these dry several days, until clear. Peel off the waxed paper, punch a hole in each shape, and add a loop of thread for hanging.

2 Make a huge stuffed shark or whale, using the method described on page 111 (tip 9). Hang this from the ceiling or prop it against a wall. Make other stuffed fish and hang them on walls around the room, or pile them in the corners of each center like schools of fish gathered in dark areas of the ocean. Your children will use them in dramatic play.

3 Make a gigantic aquarium mural. Let your children add to the display as they learn new things about underwater life. First, have children make fingerpaintings using blues, greens, violets, and yellows. Hang these close together to make the background of an underwater mural. Cut sponges into fish shapes and let your children sponge-paint fishes on the mural. Add underwater plants made from twisted green crepe-paper streamers. If desired, decorate a cereal box to resemble a pirate chest, and glue it to the board.

4 Your children can make octopuses by cutting two matching oval shapes from colored butcher paper. Glue the edges of the ovals together to make a pouch. Stuff the pouch with crumpled tissue paper before sealing it. Glue eight strips of tissue paper (in matching colors) to the back. If these octopuses are small enough, glue them to your mural. If not, punch a hole in the top of each octopus and hang these creatures from the ceiling.

5 Ask each of your children to draw his or her favorite sea creature. Mount these drawings on fish-shaped paper, and compile them into a group book. You can easily turn this into a repetitive rhyme in the style of Bill Martin's *Brown Bear, Brown Bear, What Do You See?* (Holt, 1983). As you turn each page, incorporate the picture into the rhyme. For example, "Gray whale, gray whale, what do you see? I see a yellow fish looking at me."

6 Bring in natural sponges for your children to explore. Use some for painting. Put some in the water table and others in the dramatic play area so the children can use them to wash their dishes.

7 Invite a scuba diver to visit your group and demonstrate the equipment used underwater. Have your visitor tell about what is seen under the water. Let your children try on goggles and fins.

8 Include underwater delicacies for snack. Offer children tastes of tuna, mackerel, sardines, shrimp, clams, fish sticks, or other fish. Invite families to share their favorite fish dishes with you.

9 Your children can create underwater pictures of brightly colored plants and fish. Have them use fluorescent crayons to draw their underwater scenes. Remind them to push hard on the crayons for good coverage. Next they brush on a coat of thinned blue or blue-purple tempera paint. The paint won't adhere to heavily waxed crayon surfaces, so fish and seaweed seem to move in water.

10 Set up an aquarium of tropical fish in your room. Learn the names and characteristics of each of your fish. Include scavenger fish who help keep the tank clean. Let your children help select the fish, and put clipboards of drawing paper with crayons near the tank so the children can draw what they see.